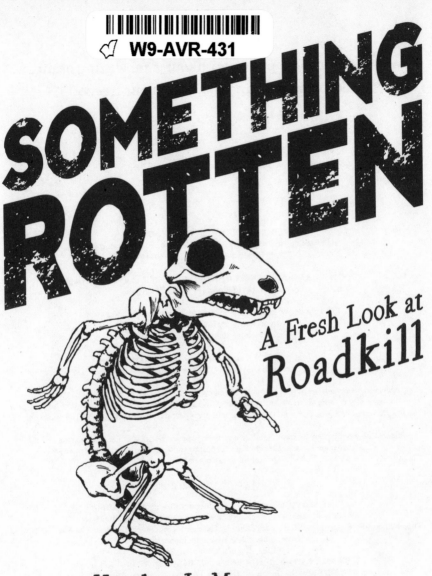

SOMETHING ROTTEN

A Fresh Look at Roadkill

Heather L. Montgomery

ILLUSTRATED BY Kevin O'Malley

BLOOMSBURY
CHILDREN'S BOOKS
NEW YORK LONDON OXFORD NEW DELHI SYDNEY

For Laddin, who put up with four-a.m. writing stints,
skunk stench, and roadkill in our freezer!

BLOOMSBURY CHILDREN'S BOOKS
Bloomsbury Publishing Inc., part of Bloomsbury Publishing Plc
1385 Broadway, New York, NY 10018

BLOOMSBURY, BLOOMSBURY CHILDREN'S BOOKS, and the Diana logo
are trademarks of Bloomsbury Publishing Plc

First published in the United States of America in October 2018
by Bloomsbury Children's Books
Paperback published in October 2019

Bloomsbury books may be purchased for business or promotional use. For information on bulk
purchases please contact Macmillan Corporate and Premium Sales Department at
specialmarkets@macmillan.com

ISBN 978-1-5476-0250-6 (paperback)

The Library of Congress has cataloged the hardcover as follows:
Names: Montgomery, Heather L., author. | O'Malley, Kevin, illustrator.
Title: Something rotten : a fresh look at roadkill / by Heather Montgomery ; illustrated by Kevin O'Malley.
Description: New York : Bloomsbury, 2018.
Identifiers: LCCN 2017056223
ISBN 978-1-68119-900-9 (hardcover) • ISBN 978-1-5476-0187-5 (e-book)
Subjects: LCSH: Roadkill—Juvenile literature. | Animal carcasses—Juvenile literature.
Classification: LCC QL49 .M79237 2018 | DDC 591.7/14—dc23
LC record available at https://lccn.loc.gov/2017056223

Book design by John Candell
Typeset by Westchester Publishing Services
Printed and bound in the U.S.A. by Berryville Graphics Inc., Berryville, Virginia
2 4 6 8 10 9 7 5 3 1

All papers used by Bloomsbury Publishing Plc are natural, recyclable products
made from wood grown in well-managed forests. The manufacturing processes
conform to the environmental regulations of the country of origin.

To find out more about our authors and books visit www.bloomsbury.com
and sign up for our newsletters.

Praise for

SOMETHING ROTTEN

An ALA Notable Book
An Orbis Pictus Recommended Book
An NCTE Notable Children's Book in the Language Arts
A Chicago Public Library Best Book

★ "The discoveries that arise from our flattened fauna will amaze you! . . . There's nothing rotten about this book—it's a keeper." —*Kirkus Reviews*, starred review

★ "An amusing, thorough overview of dead animals." —*School Library Journal*, starred review

★ "An extremely interesting treatise about roadkill and how it affects all our lives." —*School Library Connection*, starred review

"Budding naturalists or eco-activists will find it a smashing read." —*Booklist*

"Equal parts gross and cool, every science nerd will love this book! Animal-loving readers will be especially thrilled to learn how studying roadkill can prevent more casualties—and how kids are already making a difference." —Sy Montgomery, *New York Times* bestselling author and Sibert Medal–winning author of *The Hyena Scientist*

CONTENTS

A Note from Me—
the Author

This is where the magic happens," said my guide, a tanned man who looked out from under a Crocodile Dundee–style hat. He swung open the lid of a 6-foot-long white chest freezer—a freezer that reminded me of a coffin.

A skull stared up at me.

Deep black holes that once were eyes seemed to issue a challenge: *Come closer.* So I inched one tiny step forward and peeked inside the freezer.

Rotting body parts lay in a jumble: A rib cage half covered in decaying skin. Vertebrae[1] lying on their side, looking like warped crosses. A flat bone the shape of a butterfly.[2]

The bones weren't human. The bones weren't chicken or ham or beef—what you would expect to find in a freezer. The bones were from various small animals, and they filled plastic bins, open egg cartons, and orange cafeteria trays. A miniature body—now just a curled cluster of calcium[3]—nestled into one cup of an egg carton. The tidy line of its spine, the C-shaped noodles that must be ribs, and a teeny, tiny rodent skull.[4]

The bones were the reason I had hopped into my car and driven across my home state of Alabama to interview this scientist, David Laurencio. The bones, which were mostly from roadkill, were the root of my burning question: How do you use roadkill?

It might sound like an odd question, but when my curiosity takes ahold, it takes over. And on the topic of roadkill, I was way beyond curious—I was obsessed.

Every dead animal along the road stirred up questions. What *actually* happened to those animals? Does anyone ever pick them up? If so, what do they do with them? Why did the chicken/fox/deer try to cross the road in the first place? What if an animal is injured but not killed? How many animals are killed by vehicles every year? And why aren't we doing anything about it?

---

[1] *Vertebrae*: spines that form the backbone.
[2] *Sacrum*: the bone at the base of the spine to which the tailbone is attached. Reach around to the base of your back and feel yours sitting between two hard bumps on the left and right.
[3] You know, the stuff you get from milk to make your bones strong.
[4] The teeth showed that the skeleton belonged to a rodent. Rodent jaws have two big flat incisors—front teeth like a beaver's—for gnawing, a space with no teeth, and then flat molars, which are good for grinding up grain or other plant material.

My fluffy yellow dog, Piper, is my travel companion, so she heard lots and lots of questions. I wonder if she had questions too.

I didn't *want* to be asking those questions. The topic was too sad, too tragic, too disgusting to think about for very long. But I *had* been pulling my car off the road to peer at poor dead animals for years. Does my degree in biology give me an excuse for that? The death of those wild creatures was depressing, but their *bodies* were fascinating. Each carcass was an opportunity to get close to wildlife—to touch velvety bobcat fur, to wonder at the miracle of muscles inside a deer, and to run a finger over a snapping turtle's jagged spine.

For years it was like two different people waged a tug-of-war inside me—one repelled by the bloody body and one reaching toward it—until one day I gave in and let the questions take over.

That's why I was visiting David's library of dead bodies.

David is Collections Manager of Tetrapods[5] for Auburn University's Museum of Natural History. He took me to see this warm freezer, where he turned corpses into skeletal specimens that wouldn't stink, rot, or get munched on. You might be wondering why the "freezer" was warm. David had his reasons. I'll tell you about those—and the thousand or so bugs crawling all over the skeletons—in Chapter 2.

Visiting with David, I realized something: there are other people

---

[5] *Tetra* = "four"; *pod* = "foot": David handles anything with four limbs: bobcats, otters, snakes. Wait, snakes? Many snake fossils have two legs. Modern pythons grow leg bones when they are still in the shell, but the bones stop growing and become little spurs as the snake matures. But when a scientist found a four-legged fossil and called it a snake, even other scientists said, "Wait! What?" *Is* it a snake? That's still up for debate, but snakes are considered tetrapods because they came from ancient lizards.

just as intrigued by this topic. Others who find productive uses for those dead bodies. Others who care.

Little did I know then just how deep I would go—elbow deep at times—into this roadkill research.

✘ ✘ ✘

Warning:

This book is *not* for squeamish souls. It's full of lung-eating parasites,[6] ropes of intestines, and, of course, bloody bodies. The scientist in Chapter 2 who pulls squiggly things out of road-killed snakes . . . is she squeamish? No. *Disgusting* doesn't stop her.

This book is *not* for reckless readers. It's full of things you shouldn't do. Not, at least, until you are an authorized, bona fide, certified expert. I'm serious. You could catch Lyme disease, end up with a parasite in your eye, become roadkill yourself—rubber gloves can't protect you from everything.[7] The 11-year-old in Chapter 6 who rebuilt a giraffe from the bones up? He's got years of experience, his parents' support, and if he lived in the US, he'd likely need a government permit.[8]

This book is *not* for the tenderhearted: It's full of death, decay, and decomposition. And it's full of tragedy. Wildlife-vehicle

---

[6] Parasites live on or inside another creature in order to steal their food (or flesh) bit by bit.

[7] Recently, a Russian kid caught the bubonic plague from a marmot he was skinning. That's *the* plague—the one that killed off 50 million people in the fourteenth century. Because this kid got sick, 17 people had to be quarantined and 4,000 had to get vaccinated. We don't need another epidemic. I saw a picture of a guy with the plague; all that's left of his hands are crusty, blackened stumps.

[8] It might seem odd that you'd need a permit to remove a stinking carcass from the side of the road. Many places require it for certain animals; some require it for all roadkill. The US Migratory Bird Treaty Act of 1918 makes it unlawful to possess parts—including feathers—of most birds. Back when the act was created, thousands of birds were being killed for feathers for hats, so it made sense once upon a time.

collisions kill over a million animals a day. And that's just in the United States.

When I learned how many animals were dying, I wondered if we had to sit around and watch it happen. I asked even more questions, visited people who work with roadkill, and put my own hands on those bodies. While I was touring a wildlife disease center, a veterinarian student said to me: "Roadkill—it's not the end of the story."

What did she mean? What stories could roadkill tell?

So I began to let myself look (and touch and listen[9] and smell).[10] I found many others who did too. Others who, through looking directly at the tragedy, turned it into triumph: a scientist who now understands cancer better, citizens who track where wildlife cross the road, scientists who are halting extinctions, kids who make art—all thanks to roadkill.

That is what this book is about: the discoveries, ingenuity, and hope that have been inspired by roadkill.

And it all started with one squished snake . . .

---

[9] Did you know that fly maggots make a *slurch* sound? Of course, *slurch* isn't a real word, but that's onomatopoeia for you.
[10] Piper thought I should roll in it too.

CHAPTER 1
Rattled

There it was. Sprawled out on the pavement in front of me. A rattlesnake as long as my arm, with a squished midsection as wide as a car tire. So sad. As I jogged past, I wondered if the driver had aimed for the snake. Then a question hit me.

When a rattler closes his mouth, how does he not bite himself? Think about it.

His fangs are really long. Where do they go? How come they don't jab his lower lip? I mean, I knew the anatomical reason from reading a book—the fangs fold—but I still didn't *get* how.

That question grabbed ahold of me and wouldn't let go. A quarter of a mile down my little country lane, *How? How? How?* was still echoing inside my head. So I turned back around and soon I was jogging in place, staring down at the snake. There was only one way to find out.

This is the part you don't do at home. The part that even I was nervous about doing—and I'd been trained in how to safely handle snakes. The part that might be illegal—except that I had permission.[1] The part that could get me killed.

I picked it up.

Right there in the middle of the road, I bent down to pick up that rattler with my bare hands. I know, I know—I should have worn gloves. But who carries rubber gloves when they go out for a run?

Now, to look at his head, you'd never know he was dead. His eyes were staring directly at me. I had poked the snake once, twice, three times with a stick to make sure he was dead. We never expect to look into the eyes of the dead, but a rattler's eyes never close. They don't have eyelids like ours, just a clear scale that covers each eye to protect it from the claws of their prey.

I grasped firmly behind the head where his fangs couldn't reach. Even a dead rattler can bite and inject venom. His venom was still there, waiting expectantly in glands in his cheeks. His muscles were still ready to contract, waiting to squeeze those venom glands. His fangs, as finely tipped as a nurse's needle, were still sharp, waiting, waiting, waiting.

---

[1] In the United States, every state has its own rules about what you can and can't salvage from the road. Some, like California, only allow collecting for scientific purposes. Some, like Maine, have very specific laws—in order to sell a gall bladder from a road-killed bear, you have to have a hide dealer's license. Some, like Montana, make it easy: for deer, moose, elk, or antelope, all you have to do is print out a permit for each animal you take.

The only thing missing was a message from a nerve cell.

A live nerve cell actively pumps sodium ions through the cell membrane to the outside. Because the sodium ions have a positive charge, the inside of the cell is left with a negative charge. When the nerve is triggered (on a live or dead snake), the cell membrane opens and lets the sodium ions rush back in. This sends an electrical impulse to the muscles: contract! Freshly dead, this rattler's nerve cells were still primed and ready to send a message.

Very carefully, I opened his mouth. And I closed it. And I opened it and I closed it. What I had read—about him having foldable fangs—began to make sense.

With his mouth wide open, his fangs are flung out from the top jaw, right there in your face, needle sharp, raised, and ready to pierce soft skin.[2] But close the mouth, and the tips of those fangs begin to fold in, backward toward the throat.

Spring the mouth open and closed and you'll see a pink sheath, like a triangle of tissue, running from the back to the front of the top gum and down along the fang. When the mouth is open, the tissue is no longer a triangle. It's bunched up at the top of the fang like a sleeve pushed up above your elbow. The fang extends out of that tissue. As you close the jaw, that sleeve slides down to cover the curved fang and then seems to tug at it. *That must be what guides the fang*, I thought, *what eases it back into its folded position*.[3] By the time the mouth is closed all but a whisper, the fangs have vanished.

---

[2] There are 2 fangs—I always thought there were ones in the lower jaw, too, but I was wrong. The snake can choose to use just 1. Why? Maybe his prey is a small animal and only requires 1, or maybe the risk of breaking a tooth is just too great. If something goes wrong, he can't run to the dentist.

[3] Hinged bones in the skull work together to swing the fang into place.

I opened the mouth again and noticed something strange, something that looked like a little slit. It wasn't the esophagus, which was a normal-looking hole at the very back of his mouth. This slit was in the center of the floor of his mouth.

My degree was in general biology, not herpetology,[4] so I'd never studied snake anatomy. The questions came boiling out of me. What is that? Why is it there? Is it normal? Why don't I have one? Do all snakes have those? I *had* to know.

Here is the second thing you shouldn't try yourself.

Now, I can deal with gross stuff, but spit wigs me out. So it took some nerve, but I stuck my pinkie into that rattler's mouth.

The floor of the mouth was gushy—like mine would feel, I guess, to a giant poking his finger in my mouth—but that little slit wasn't. In fact, it felt kind of hard. Under the flesh was a tube, as if the slit were the end of a miniature PVC pipe.

But where did it go? And what was it for? Did it lead to the stomach? Where?

I *had* to know.

So I did yet another thing you shouldn't do. I carried that rattler home, got out

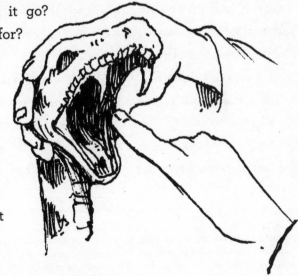

---

[4] *Herpetology:* the study of amphibians and reptiles.

my scissors and gloves, and sliced the snake right down the middle.

It was *so gross*—guts and blood and muscles everywhere—and *so cool* at the same time. I could see his entire digestive system (the esophagus, stomach, intestines, and, yeah, the other end too), his circulatory system (although some of the veins and arteries had been destroyed), and his muscles!

But what I most wanted to figure out was: Where does that pipe go? So I found it up in the neck. I put my finger on it and followed it through that gushy stuff until it came to a lung. A lung?

Hmmm...

Think about how a snake eats. When we eat, we cut our food up into civilized little bites, we chew, and we swallow. But a snake doesn't have a fork and a knife. He opens that jaw wide, wide, wide and consumes his dinner in one looooooong gulp.[5] To swallow a baby bunny, it could take this snake a while. Now, imagine I shoved a burger the size of a backpack down your throat.

How would you breathe?

If a snake's anatomy were like yours, he'd suffocate. Luckily, he's got this smooth little tube that acts like a snorkel. The tube is his windpipe, and the end of it—the slit I had seen—is called the glottis. Whenever he's got some bunny crammed in his mouth, the glottis pops out to the corner of his mouth to let him breathe.

Cool!

---

[5] Unlike all the legends you have heard, his jaw doesn't unhinge. The connection between his upper and lower jaws is super-flexible—it can extend to 130 degrees, while ours can only do a wimpy 30 degrees. Parts of his skull flex too. Unlike ours, his left and right lower jaws aren't firmly connected to each other. To get food into his throat, he thrusts his lower jaw forward one side at a time, "walking" it up the prey, then slips his backwardly curved teeth into the meat, and pulls the rest of his mouth, head, and body onto his food.

But that wasn't the only intriguing thing. This tube led to just 1 lung. Where was the other lung? I fished through the body parts. Nothing. I checked the ground at my feet. Empty. I gave Piper a questioning look. She was a good dog, lying there in the shade, thumping her bushy yellow tail when I turned her way. No bloody evidence on her lips.

This snake had only 1 lung.

What?

Maybe I had found a snake with a unique birth defect. A teenage mutant ninja snake?

I ran inside, washed my hands, and sat down to email a herpetologist. This was *amazing.* I would ship this specimen to him overnight. It was probably the only snake in the entire world with just 1 lung. He would put it on display in a national museum. I would be famous!

But right before I hit send, I decided to do a bit more research—always, always, always a wise choice. I pulled out all my snake books. I dug in. I discovered something that made me sit right down on the floor.

All rattlesnakes have just 1 working lung.[6] *What?* Obviously, there was a lot I didn't know about snake anatomy. One of the really cool things about nature is that there are always more amazing things

---

[6] Technically, they do have 2 lungs, but the left one is vestigial, meaning that it is a leftover, nonfunctioning remnant.

out there to discover. How do snakes survive with only 1 lung? Why do they *have* only 1 working lung?[7] And how had I missed that fun fact before? Imagine how embarrassed I would have been if I had clicked send on that email!

All this made me wonder: If I could discover this much from looking at one animal that had died on the asphalt, what were other people learning from roadkill?

---

[7] My guess is that ambush predators (like rattlers, who sit and wait for their prey instead of cruising around all day looking for it) require less oxygen. If they don't need all that oxygen, why waste the space (there's not much of it in that long, thin body) and energy on a second lung?

CHAPTER 2
Library of Life

David Laurencio pulled open the door—not any normal door, but a mass that looked like it had been carved straight from the 6-inch-thick wall. It felt like we were stepping into a bank vault: cold, emotionless cement floor, walls, and ceiling. The steel shut with a clunk, and then we were inside a library of dead bodies.

Rows of metal shelving surrounded us. Each shelf was crammed with tall jars capped in black, chrome, or white lids. Bottles were stuffed full of bodies—scaly or smooth or shelled. Ropes of snakes, one coil stacked upon another. A milky-white lens peered at me with a somewhat accusing look.

That copperhead couldn't strike me now. So I took a closer look, noticing the shape of his scales. The belly scales of the copperhead were wide, each one spanning the belly like a rung on a ladder, while the rest were narrow and ran up the back like shingles on a roof.

We were inside the wet collections[1] of the Auburn University Museum of Natural History. This is not the place to go if you are looking for kid-friendly games, beautiful artwork, or cheery displays. No, this is a working museum—one designed for the scientifically minded. David was showing me how roadkill saves lives.

Earlier in the spring, when I had met David at a herpetology conference, he pulled a tray of Dead on Road, or DOR, animals out of the trunk of his car. A gray tree frog that had suction-cup toes and bright yellow thighs. A diamondback water snake that people frequently accuse of being a water moccasin. The animals smelled like a biology lab. Other scientists had collected those bodies, preserved them, and turned them over to David. Each DOR would become one of the 40,000 specimens in the amphibians and reptiles room of the museum. A whole network of folks across the southeast regularly collect DOR animals for the museum.

What do they do if the animal is really squashed and nasty?

"If they get to be 'snake-ment,' where they are part of the pavement," David said, "we just do a photo voucher.[2] If it is completely

---

[1] A "wet collection" is just what it sounds like: full of liquid. Snakes, salamanders, and fish are all preserved in alcohol. Alcohol is combustible, so the collection has to be surrounded by fire walls. That's why the room felt like a vault. It sounds pretty safe, but David spends lots of time on the *inside* of those walls—with all his babies and the potential for an explosion!

[2] The museum staff or volunteers take digital photos of every specimen that comes in. The preservatives are great at stopping rot, but not so good for color.

mangled but fresh, we can still get DNA[3] from the muscle tissue. We try to record the sex and get as much data from it as we can."

To David, data is everything. Data = information, and all kinds of data are associated with a museum specimen: where it was found, when it was found, who found it, how it was killed . . .

"We've had to lock our freezers because people keep throwing snakes in there with no data," David said. "They're just taking up space. Worthless, scientifically. The password? Data."

A toe tag. Well, the tag wasn't on the lizard's toe—it was tied around his belly—but from all the detective TV shows I've watched, that's what I'd call it. The number on the tag is recorded in a database where all the specimens' data is stored. David was holding up a big jar packed with lizards instead of pickles. It was *so cool* to be standing in the middle of all those animals, but what, I wondered, do scientists need so many specimens for? Wouldn't one green anole[4] be enough?

With his pinkie, David pointed out dots on a map in a book about Alabama reptiles and amphibians. On the page about green anoles,

---

[3] *DNA*: deoxyribonucleic acid. DNA is a chemical code in every living cell that contains information about how to grow and function.

[4] A smooth-skinned lizard that can change from bright leafy green to dark, bark brown. You might think it's a chameleon, but it's not. It is America's own color magician. Anoles have three pigments—xanthophores (yellow), melanophores (brown), and cyanophores (blue)—that move up or down in the skin, creating different colors depending on the lizard's temperature or stress level. Imagine if you turned bright green when a test question stressed you out. Embarrassing!

the dots showed where they live. But David has also shown me his own copy of the book. It's sprinkled with colorful dots he's added as specimens have come in—animals that didn't read the book, and lived outside of the boundaries humans had drawn on maps. All those books, encyclopedias, websites that tell us where an animal lives? That info has to come from somewhere. David and his library of death are ground zero.

"Herpers[5] tend to be pretty competitive," David told me. "To get to find an animal in a county—or better yet, a state—for the first time gives you some bragging rights."

There's this guy, Jimmy Stiles, who takes road trips at midnight just to add dots to David's map. As he told me about a rainy night when he went road cruising, Jimmy said, "I was really hoping to find some dead ones." It might seem odd that someone who loves these animals so much hopes to find them dead. But that day in the museum demonstrated just how valuable those dead bodies are.

"Museums are warehouses of biological data. How do you know what a snake eats, right? You could either follow a snake around for 50 years or you could go to a museum and look at some stomachs. At the museum, you might see 50–100 snakes, and the nice thing is that they have been collected over time and space." David was so excited, he was talking with his hands. "You get a lot more information from looking at the variation."

Then David made a leap to a *really* big idea about why collecting natural history data is so important.

"Any ecological work that is going to be done with this group is

---

[5] *Herpers*: a nickname for people who are into herpetology (amphibians and reptiles).

completely based on the natural history we know: when they reproduce, what they eat, when they eat, how big they get, what habitat they need. Do they live all over the forest? Do they live only near ponds?

"Say Florida panthers are in danger. What do we do? For conservation, there is a series of steps we take, based off ... what? What they eat. What habitat they need, when they reproduce. Their natural history. This is a ridiculous example, but if we started throwing a bunch of cabbages out into the field to feed mountain lions, that is not going to do any good."

✗ ✗ ✗

David and I toured the fish, insect, and plant sections, but he couldn't help himself; he kept showing me more herp stuff.

For example, there were these oversized coolers. A graduate student named Melissa had used them to haul snakes back from Florida.

"Melissa is looking at pentastomes."

Penta-what?

"To do that," David kept going, "she needs to look at snake lungs."

Wait! Someone else—a real scientist—was digging around in snake lungs? I *needed* to meet her.

Melissa wasn't there that day, so I tracked her down later. I wanted see just how she cut open a snake. To know what a pentastome was. And to learn what it had to do with snake lungs. I was desperately curious to know more, but we ended up playing email tag for months. Would I miss out? Her email response: *I still have a ton of snakes to get through, so no worries about missing out on the guts and gore* ☺.

All right!

When I finally made it to her lab, Melissa was ready and waiting with her special scissors, a metal tray, and a road-killed cottonmouth in a plastic bag. The dissection didn't disappoint. *C-r-r-unch.* Melissa clipped her way through snake tissue. She peeled back the skin, muscles, and other gunk to reveal a pink honeycomb-like lung.

But the really good stuff was the wormy-like things she found inside, clues for solving a red-hot mystery of nature.

All around Everglades National Park in Florida, snakes had been popping up with parasites in their lungs. Those were the pentastomes David had mentioned. Pentastomes are odd little guys also called tongue worms. They don't attack tongues, thank goodness, but there are plenty of other weird facts about them.[6] Like the fact that they eat by slurping up blood from their hosts.[7] The fact that they spend their lives inside not 1 but at least 2 different hosts. Or that, although scientists have been debating it for years (and still aren't sure), we think that these guys are close cousins to fish lice.[8]

---

[6] They are called tongue worms because another kind of pentastome looks like a tongue.

[7] *Hosts*: animals who would rather not have these parasites as guests.

[8] Yes, fish lice are real. They aren't real lice, though. They are related to barnacles—those

What we do know about pentastomes is that there are around 140 species and most live out their adult lives in the lungs of reptiles. When the female lays eggs, the snake coughs them up out of the lung. If the snake then swallows them, they go all the way through the snake's guts and then squish out with the feces. *Plop!* Those little eggs are accidentally gobbled up by a fish, a mammal, a frog, or some other unsuspecting little creature whose food is smeared with the teeny, tiny eggs.[9] That animal becomes the intermediate host for the parasite. Inside the intermediate host, the egg hatches and the larva[10] goes to work. It has these little hooks on its head to claw its way right through the host's gut wall. The larva doesn't kill its host; it hunkers down as a cyst to wait it out, hoping that the intermediate host will get gobbled up by—you guessed it—a snake. Then the cycle starts all over again.

So, what does all that have to do with Melissa, her scissors, and a mystery? I'll give you the short version of the story. For a couple of summers, Melissa had been collecting native[11] snakes that had unfortunately been killed on the road. One day, when she cut a snake open . . .

. . . there was a parasite.

Ever since another scientist had tipped her off to the presence of pentastomes inside another kind of snake in the Everglades, Melissa had been on the lookout for those little bloodsuckers.

"At first it was a garter snake I found it in. I was like, *Wow!*" As

---

things that stick onto the sides of boats—and happen to think fish scales and mucus are tasty.

[9] Or a coprophage—an animal that eats poop on purpose.

[10] You know, like with insect metamorphosis. A caterpillar is the larval stage of a butterfly. Except these larvae aren't quite as cute ☺.

[11] *Native*: an organism that lived there originally.

she talked, Melissa's fingers, decked out in blue lab gloves, shot up and out like fireworks.

What's the big deal? Parasites (ticks, fleas, etc.) live on and in tons of animals—including you! The big deal was that Melissa found lots and lots and *lots* of tongue worms in all kinds of snakes' lungs. In lots of native snakes' lungs. More pentastomes than there ever should be.

Did I tell you that these pentastomes can be up to 3 inches long?[12] How would you like a bunch of them slurping around in your lungs?

The mystery: Where were they all coming from?

Some likely villains were lurking in the swamps of the Everglades. Some 10-foot-long villains: Burmese pythons![13] You may have heard about these exotic[14] guys. They aren't just any old snakes doing what snakes do. They originated in Asia, were brought to Florida as pets, and were accidentally or intentionally released into the wild.[15] Because no native critters can tackle these big boys, they are taking over the neighborhood, munching up all the bunnies, raccoons, bobcats, deer, and even alligators![16]

What if, Melissa hypothesized, stealing everyone else's lunch wasn't the only thing pythons were up to? What if they were secretly infesting the native snakes with pentastomes? Now, they wouldn't do it intentionally, but how can they help it if the eggs they poop

---

[12] The boys are much smaller (less than half an inch), so those mega-long ones must have been lady 'stomes.

[13] One monster python found in the Everglades was 18 feet long!

[14] *Exotic*: an organism brought in from another place; the opposite of native.

[15] When your cute little pet snake outgrows its aquarium, your bedroom, and your backyard, you have to do something with it. But set it free in the wild, and all of nature will be mad at you.

[16] When one python was dragged out of the swamp, it had 12 deer hooves in its belly, weighed 105 pounds, and was ready to poop out 14 pounds of bones, teeth, and hair. And just think—we don't even know how many of these big guys are out there!

out happen to end up in the very same food that other snakes swallow for dinner?

But that, of course, was all just a hypothesis, and one thing you should know about science is that it's all about evidence.

The first thing Melissa had to do was track down what species of pentastome she had found. By just looking at them, it's hard to tell different species apart. Using a microscope helps, but even that's not enough. You've got to go all the way down to the DNA.[17]

So Melissa got busy extracting DNA. To do that she put pieces of pentastome tissue the size of a period [.] in a chemical mixture. Then she spun the samples using a machine called a vortex, let them incubate on a heat block, and spun them some more. She siphoned off the top layer (with fingers crossed that it contained the DNA). The amount of DNA was teeny tiny, so she used a special procedure to make more of it. Then she put a high-tech machine and ultraviolet light to work, and searched for a bright glowing band to let her know she'd captured the right DNA. She shipped off frozen vials of the sample to a company who sent her back a graph of colorful humps and bumps and a long string of letters: AGGACACAAT... which she uploaded into some software called Geneious.[18] Once she made sense of the code, Melissa checked out GenBank, a digital library chock-full of DNA data.

---

[17] DNA is made of 4 different bases, represented by the letters A, G, T, and C. The sequence of those letters is different in every living thing on the planet. However, a string of DNA contains sections called genes, which work together as a unit to determine something like eye color. All animals in the same species have the same genes, but the sequence of bases within those genes will be slightly different.
[18] Clever name for gene-sequencing software!

<u>To Do List</u>

1. What is this weirdo?

✓Check! She found a match in the database. The parasite's name is *Raillietiella orientalis*. What a mouthful. Let's use its nickname, *R. orientalis*.

<u>To Do List</u>

✓ 1. What is this weirdo?
2. Is it native?

Next, Melissa needed to find out if *R. orientalis* could be native to North America. Maybe the native snakes had infected the pythons with the tongue worms?

To figure that out, Melissa, a small army of volunteers, and a heap of college students had to get clever. For 4 years, volunteers across Florida, Alabama, and Georgia picked up just about every road-killed snake they could find. Melissa and the students checked 483 of them for pentastomes. They also obtained pentastomes that had been pulled out of the lungs of 1,049 Burmese pythons.[19] If *R. orientalis* belongs in North America, you would expect to find it in snakes across the entire region. But they didn't find *R. orientalis* outside of the python range in Florida. As we looked at a map, it was pretty obvious to us who the culprit was.

---

[19] Some from roadkill but mostly from official python removal programs. It's a sad thing to have to kill an animal, but the government looked at how those exotics were decimating the ecosystem, and made the hard choice to put the animals down. It's not an easy job, so lots of groups are helping. For example, the South Florida Water Management District paid python hunters $49,504 to eliminate 158 pythons who, if stretched tongue to tail, would reach higher than the Empire State Building.

But the plot thickened.

"Doing the dissections," Melissa said, "I started noticing 1, 2, or 3 of these in a python. Sometimes I would find 20 or 30 in a native snake's lung."

In one native snake, they found 76!

I thought about that as I watched her poke her gloved finger into the body cavity of the cottonmouth.

"Oh," she said, her voice jumping an octave in delight. "There's one!" She sounded like a mom proudly pointing out one of her children on the ball field.

"Oh my . . ." I muttered, pointing. "So that is one. Is that one too?"

"Uh-huh."

"Is that one *and* that one?" I asked.

"Right." She had picked a winner. I could see four already. Balled up in the lung, they looked like thick boogers, but laid out on the lab tray, they  were like skinny ramen noodles. Damp, white, clingy.

The team had found the parasite in 13 of the 26 snake species native to the Everglades. That's half of them! Melissa started crunching the numbers and discovered something really troubling. In comparison to the pythons, the native snakes: 1) were more likely to have tongue worms, 2) had more tongue worms, and 3) had larger tongue worms.

You'd think that more pentastomes in the native snakes would mean that the parasites started out in the natives, but you'd be wrong. Deep inside a lung, pentastomes ooze out a chemical to cover their cuticle[20]—kind of like an invisibility cloak—so that the snake's immune system can't "see" them. But when a parasite and a snake species have been waging a war against each other for, like, forever, the snake's system has figured out ways to uncloak the parasite. Pythons haven't defeated the pentastomes, but their immune systems can keep the parasites' numbers in check. When, however, a parasite is introduced to a new host (like a garter snake), the sneaky little buggers can grow like crazy.

Now Melissa's data were starting to make sense.

When I leaned in close to the cottonmouth to use my magnifier, I could see dark matter inside the parasites—their guts were full of blood.

"A female pentastome is basically a tube for eating and digestion, plus a very long tube for egg production," Melissa explained. "One species can put out 3,000 eggs a day."[21]

What?

To Do List

✓ 1. What is this weirdo?

✓ 2. Is it native? *No!*

3. Who else is it munching on?

Melissa is still tracking down the full life cycle of *R. orientalis*. She thinks it goes through the snake and then more than one

---

[20] *Cuticle*: protective covering. Typically these are hard and waxy—but not in pentastomes. They just *have* to be different.

[21] Over an entire lifetime (which could be 7 years), a single tongue worm might produce several million eggs. Watch out, reptiles!

intermediate host. What clued her in to that? Another scientist found that many of the snakes infected with *R. orientalis* feed on frogs. Most of the Florida natives who were infected also feed on frogs. One problem: Burmese pythons eat lots of critters, but frogs? Not so much. So the life cycle can't go: snake → frog → snake. There's probably a third host involved, but it's still a big question mark in Melissa's mind.

<u>To Do List</u>
✓ 1. What is this weirdo?
✓ 2. Is it native? *No!*
✗ 3. Who else is it munching on?
   4. How does it affect living snakes?

People kept asking Melissa what impact the parasites were having on the native snakes. "Well, at the very least, they are sucking nutrients out of the host."

Surely, 76 little buggers in there would make it hard to breathe. Perhaps the parasites slow the snakes down, especially when they need to move fast. They were found as roadkill, after all. Next on Melissa's to do list? Snag some living snakes and put them into a metabolic chamber. That instrument will let her see just how hard a snake is "working" to do normal things. She wants to compare infected and noninfected snakes. What will she discover? Who knows?[22] Melissa and the hordes of other scientists out there have a few more mysteries yet to solve.

---

[22] Curious scientists tossed a bunch of pentastome-infected geckos into a metabolic chamber. The parasites didn't really affect geckos that had been couch potatoes. But ones that had been running around? The more pentastomes they had, the harder their bodies were working.

When we were done playing with his insides, Melissa coiled up the cottonmouth and flipped him right side up. Then she settled him into a natural-looking pose and said, "Cottonmouths are so cool. They are just such pretty snakes."

What do you do with the hundreds and hundreds of snakes you've cut open? You add them to the museum's collection, of course. They won't go to waste.

On my earlier trip to the museum, David had pointed to jars and jars that contained stomach contents pulled from Melissa's snakes. Picking through the stomachs, someone had spotted blue bones—a young Cuban tree frog—inside the tummy of a Florida native snake. That was a valuable discovery. Those nonnative tree frogs had also invaded the Everglades, and this was our first clue that a native snake had been doing its best to keep their population in check.

As David had walked me into the dry collections;[23] it smelled of mothballs. There were drawers and drawers of skulls and pelts. A shelf shouting with the colors of parrots and parakeets. A student studying trapdoor spiders.[24] A kaleidoscope of shells. A 4-inch-thick scientific logbook. Insects glued to the tips of triangles of paper. Boxes and boxes of skeletons.[25]

How do you go from rotting roadkill to showy skeletons?

That's where the warm freezer comes in.

For the grand finale of my tour, David took me outside to see the dermestid beetle colony. Dermestid beetles think dead flesh is

---

[23] Everything that isn't kept in alcohol.
[24] The spider butts look like Aztec coins and are used like shields to seal up the entrance to the spiders' lairs.
[25] This place must be *tons of fun* on Halloween!

yummy. Give them a dead body, and they gobble up the skin, blood, guts, muscles, brains . . . and leave the bones behind. But there's a little problem with having skin-hungry insects in your museum. If they get into the collection, bye-bye fuzzy bear fur. So the beetles get their own private suite out back, locked in a sealed closet, comfy in a coffin-shaped deep freezer. Their thermostat is set at between 78 and 80 degrees Fahrenheit—nice and toasty for baby beetles.

David raised the freezer lid.

A whiff hit me, almost like when a dead mouse has been caught in the heater, but not quite that strong. It was kind of soft and sweet, nothing like the stench I'd expected from all those body parts. An eyeless skull stared at me. The orange trays were covered in little black dots. There were thousands of beetles in there.

The beetles aren't large—just the size of a sunflower seed—but they are mighty. And the kid beetles actually do most of the hard work. The 6-legged larva chomp, chomp, chomp away, swallowing everything but bone.

It takes work to keep each bat, rat, or bobcat connected to its data as its flesh gets eaten off. Dermestid beetles munch paper, too, so toe tags are no good. Plus, the beetle larva will drag the bodies around if you let them, so animals are separated in the cups of egg cartons, each with a metal tag like a military dog tag.

Sprit, sprit, sprit. David misted the area with water. The smell jumped up about 20 notches,[26] but he had to keep those little buggers happy.

---

[26] No one knows for sure why it gets smellier when you add water, but recently scientists have used high-speed cameras to study the smell of rain, and they might have an explanation. When raindrops land on soil or porous surfaces (rotting flesh, in this case), air trapped under the raindrop bubbles up and sprays out tiny particles. Once airborne, the particles are free to float up to your nose.

"We try to only put new things in on Fridays so we have the weekend for the smell to go away."

As I left the museum, my nose was filled with odors, my heart with wonder, and my mind with more questions. You know how sometimes you go someplace like a zoo for the first time and you don't realize how big it is? After half the day you've seen 1/10 of what they have, and then you kind of panic because you want to see it all but you also don't want to leave the lions?

That's how I was beginning to feel about roadkill. I didn't want to leave the museum, but if David and the folks at that one museum were using roadkill in so many fascinating ways, what might other scientists be doing?

CHAPTER 3

Dead Discoveries

Three kettles[1] of vultures swirled above my head in an ocean of blue sky. All those scavengers for one coyote who happened to have black fur? Spying on them through my binoculars, I thought: *His meat must be tasty.* But when I hiked to the coyote's body halfway down the hill in my pasture, the only thing missing was his eyes. What? Were they all being polite, waiting for the other guy to go first?[2]

In case you are wondering, that wasn't a typing mistake: the coyote really was black, not tan or brown or gray or agouti[3] like every other coyote I'd ever seen. When I had spotted him dead on the road 4 days before, the shape, size, and color didn't add up. *Black,* I

---

[1] Kettle: a group of birds swirling together in the air. The day before, I had counted 71 vultures up there!

[2] Turns out, vultures don't really like to chow down on coyotes (or other predators—go figure). Like a kid pushing her broccoli around on her dinner plate, they put it off, hoping that something tastier will come along.

[3] Agouti: each hair is banded with different dark and light colors.

thought. *It must be a dog, or maybe a fox—hadn't I read something about black foxes?* But as I backed my car up to it, I saw the face and scrawny body and knew it had to be a coyote.

Weird.

That wasn't the reason I loaded that stinky body into my car. As I settled him down into Piper's spot in the backseat, I had been hoping he'd help me figure out this question: After an animal gets hit, what actually happens to the body? But as I drove home, as I stumbled under his weight when I was carrying him down the hill, as Piper stood off to the side, not willing to come too close,[4] the *Why is he black?* question started taking over.

The questions seemed to fight for my attention like cartoon characters climbing on top of one another, each trying to block the other from my sight. The *What actually happens?* question seemed so gruesomely intriguing, like it might lead me down some dark and windy road. But after some quick searching on the internet, the *Why is he black?* question looked like it led straight up a cliff to what could be an interesting view.

I love conquering a tough climb, so I picked up the phone and dialed Dr. Bridgett vonHoldt at Princeton University. It's only fair I warn you: Bridgett's research is complicated, her conclusions are controversial, and, to tell you the truth, the implications kind of blew my mind.

Turns out, that black coyote was something special, and it had something to do with a much bigger story about canine hybridization.[5] The canines are an entire family of animals—dogs, wolves,

---

[4] Smart dog—the poor coyote was hopping with fleas.
[5] *Hybridization*: when 2 different kinds of animals breed with each other.

foxes, coyotes—which are closely related, and many of them can interbreed. When I started asking around about a black coyote, Dr. vonHoldt told me: "It is a quite rare and prized animal. I only see about 1 per 120 coyotes every year in Pennsylvania."

Bridgett is a cat lover, but she's been making some shocking discoveries about dogs. Bridgett is also an identical twin. She *says* that has nothing to do with her obsession with DNA, but I'm not so sure . . .

And honestly, I didn't really understand why folks were so obsessed with DNA. I mean, you can't pet DNA; you can't trace it through an animal like you can that cool snake snorkel; *you can't even see* it. But Bridgett was pretty jazzed about it, and so were David and Melissa and a few more folks you haven't met yet. Plus, it did help solve that pentastome mystery. I had started this tough climb, so I guessed I'd better finish it.

In an email, Bridgett filled me in about a mutation that caused some coyotes to be black. A mutation is when there's a mistake in the copying of DNA, and something gets all flip-flopped around (think: *pea* becomes *pee*). Because the code word then reads differently, it can change something as major as the color of an entire animal.

"The mutation originally occurred in dogs, and is old. It, at some point, was transferred into the coyote species," Bridgett explained. How long ago? No one knows for sure, but that's just the kind of question that gets her pumped up, and Bridgett is just the kind of person who will keep digging until she finds a bone.

I had gotten the idea that this black coyote could make a contribution to science, and that is why I headed back down the big hill in my pasture toward that canine carcass.

In my bag:

- measuring tape
- gloves
- plastic baggies
- data-recording sheet
- scissors

The chill February wind whisked away the bad smell for the most part, but when the wind stalled for a moment, that deep earthy, rotting smell seeped into my sinuses. I decided to make it fast, but then I couldn't. There was so much to look at.

The grass was matted down 3 feet in every direction. Shiny blue-bottle flies zipped and darted. Crusty white splotches surrounded the carcass. A few dark downy feathers drenched and bedraggled like wet cotton stuck to his fur. From turkey vultures?[6]

---

[6] Did you know that when vultures go to the bathroom, they pee right down their legs? It probably cools them off, and the ammonia in the urine might sanitize their feet, which squish and squash through all kinds of nasty.

Who else had been here?

The coyote's gums were drying out, blackening, and turning to taffy. I shuddered and reached for them. The assignment I had agreed to was going to be grisly.

Bridgett was the primary investigator for the Canine Ancestry Project. Its goal: to understand how North American canines are related to each other. To do this, they needed DNA from 50 canines in every state. She didn't have a *single one* from Alabama. That black coyote was just waving his tail to volunteer for her study.

I had been sent specific instructions: "The key is to make sure the conical tube is filled to the 2-mL line with beads, and add a pea-size piece of tissue." The conical tube was a plastic vial full of pearl-colored silica beads.[7] The tissue she wanted?

Tongue.

Turns out that for people who work with dead coyotes (trappers, scientists, and weirdos like me), the tongue is an easy place to grab some DNA. Only about 5 percent of her samples came from roadkill; most came from "pest" management. When Bridgett realized that states were having competitions because people saw coyotes as pests—killing thousands a year—[8]she wondered if there was a way to at least have *something* positive come out of all that killing.

It was those tongue bits that had given her the data for her surprising conclusions. But I should start at the beginning. For

---

[7] Silica sucks up moisture and keeps the flesh from rotting. It's like those little packets that come in your shoe box. You can reuse them to preserve your baseball cards, dry out flowers, or revive a cell phone that's been dropped in water.

[8] In 1 year in the eastern United States, coyotes killed more than $20 million worth of cattle, so you can see why some folks call them pests.

decades, scientists have been working to sort out a few things about canines.

Long, long ago, coyotes hung out only in the Central Plains of North America, but now they've spread to Central America and eastern North America. We knew they were related to, but different from, wolves. Though we didn't know exactly how, or why, you find them only in certain places.

We also knew that over 100 years ago, coyotes jumped the Mississippi River and headed east. Well, they didn't actually jump the river and they didn't actually head due east. A northern front of coyotes moved across the Great Lakes region and into the northeastern United States. A southern front moved through the southern states and all the way into Florida. If you look at a map, it looks like they were running right around the ends of the Appalachian Mountains—hey, that kind of makes sense.

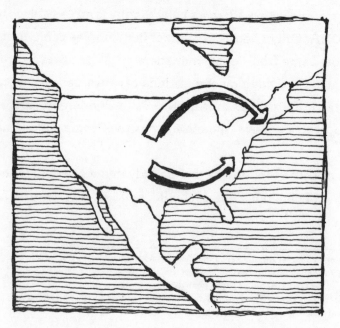

Then the Atlantic Ocean got in their way, so the coyotes started traveling along the East Coast. The northerners headed toward the sunny south, and the southerners headed up north. What would happen when they met? A great big family reunion with watermelon, corn on the cob, and homemade ice cream? Okay, I might be getting a bit carried away here. Bridgett took a more scientific approach.

"The first question to tackle was trying to understand the differences we see from the south to the north." Bridgett and her team had studied over 400 hunks of tongues[9] from Florida to New York.

What did she discover? Those two groups look pretty different.

Remember my black coyote? Part of my job was to measure all the parts. But how? Thankfully, months before, I had watched a video of a scientist and veterinarian students[10] measuring a DOR wolf from Turkey. The scientist was speaking a language I couldn't understand, but a measuring tape makes sense in any language, so I had learned how to do it.

I wrapped the measuring tape around the chest of that black coyote—not a pleasant job, as the bones crunched inside when I lifted it up. I kept going, though, knowing that the data could be an important addition to what southern coyotes "look" like to a scientist.[11]

"If you capture a coyote in Florida," Bridgett had said, "they are

---

[9] To be honest, all the samples weren't from tongues. Scientists also sent in samples like scat, hair, and toenail clippings from live coyotes—they weren't slicing live tongues off!

[10] The vet students were learning how those animals are put together.

[11] In addition to the chest girth at the armpits, I was a good little research assistant and recorded the width and length of the skull, distance between the eyes, the left ear height (16.5 cm!), rear hock to toe, footpad width and length, and body length from shoulder to base of tail. And its gender, location, which dewclaws it had, color, any visible disease (none, thank goodness), and that it was DOR. Whew!

about a 25-pound animal. It looks like a typical coyote. Small and narrow and has that distinct coyote look.

"If you go up in Maine or Nova Scotia or Vermont, the coyotes will be upwards of 2 to 3 times the size. Easily a 50–60-pound animal."

No little scrawny canine there. Why?

Those northern coyotes "may have mingled a little too intensely with the wolves and produced some puppies between a wolf and a coyote. And the hybrid pups might have stayed with the coyote mother and grown up as coyotes," Bridgett explained. "So they are genetically different and they are visually different and they are even ecologically different from the coyotes of the south."

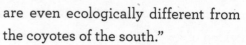

But a coyote is a coyote, right?[12]

"What we are trying to figure out is: Where are these 2 fronts meeting and how much mixing are they doing?"

That was neat, but not too surprising, complicated, or controversial. It was the next statement that got my heart beating faster. Doesn't it always feel like the stuff in science books happened at least a hundred years ago? Like all the good stuff has already been discovered? Well, not this time!

---

[12] Piper loves to howl like a coyote. But howling isn't the only thing coyotes do. They also yip, yelp, bark, huff, wail, growl, and squeal. I wonder if they ever get hoarse.

"And that," Bridgett went on, "is something that is just happening in the past 10 years."

"*Real-ly?*" I said, my voice breaking over those two syllables. This is happening right now. In our lifetimes! This is where I had gotten fired up about the idea that the black coyote, *my* black coyote, had something to contribute.

Bridgett totally got that. She was all excited about making discoveries happen today, tomorrow, and every day after that, but then I heard her let out a deep sigh. And this is where the mind-blowing part of the story comes in.

The part that I'm not really sure how to feel about.

The part that she sounded reluctant to tell me.

"This is a very frustrating time for me. The mixing between the north and south appears to occur in a very narrow geographic region in North Carolina." The very same place that, coincidentally, red wolves have been reintroduced back into the wild. The *endangered* red wolves.

Once, I did a presentation about how people were working to rescue red wolves,[13] so I knew their story. Because they had been disappearing from the face of the planet, a huge effort had been made by the US government to capture some, let them breed in a safe place, and release them back into one region of North Carolina. Hundreds of people have worked to save the red wolves from going extinct.[14]

But it hasn't been working. Even with all that effort, Bridgett said

---

[13] "Red" wolves aren't necessarily red. They can be any combination of yellow, black, gray, brown, and red.

[14] Red wolves and their fuzz-ball pups are on the critically endangered list—a list that should have flashing red lights and nasty-sounding horns going off in your mind.

the wild population of red wolves in North Carolina is down to fewer than 50 animals. Not enough to be able to sustain themselves as a population.

"Which is a very big problem in my mind." I was nodding as Bridgett rapidly told the story. "Many of the red wolves have been, uh, well..."

Across the miles of phone lines, I could almost see her face contorting as she tried to figure out how to say the next part.

"Much of the red wolf genetics are similar to coyote genetics. And because you are talking to me, I will tell you my perspective. The work that we've done has pretty much identified that the red wolf genes are a unique combination of coyote genes predominantly with some mixture of wolf genes."

"What?" I blurted out rudely.

Her words slowed down. "Which then means"—I heard her breath come out in a huff—"that the red wolf...is not...a separate...species."

I blinked, trying to take *that* in.

"Based solely on the genetics, red wolves are not a unique North American species. That is not what we have found evidence for."

Bridgett's words sped up again. "Which is okay, because we are learning about wolves and coyotes and how they breed with each other—which is very readily. And this produces a much larger question that we have to ask, which is: How do we define a species?"[15]

---

[15] How do you define a species? Is it really if 2 animals will interbreed or not? Or maybe it should be how similar or different they look or act? Or how different their DNA is? But if so, where do you draw the line—0.02 percent, 0.2 percent, 2 percent, 20 percent? And who gets to make that decision?

I was eager to hear everything else Bridgett was saying, but my mind was still stuck on the words *not a separate species.* How can that be? Red wolves are red wolves, right? Think of the controversy that could happen over an endangered species that is not a separate species.

This right here, this big idea, was why I was willing to grab that coyote's taffy-looking gums, to put my fingers in his mouth with the thing that disgusts me the most—spit—and to snip out a piece of coyote tongue.[16] But it also felt like a kick in the gut. My "belief" that a red wolf was a unique species was being put into question. This is science. Science based on evidence. I wonder if that's how people felt when Aristotle started providing evidence that the Earth wasn't flat.

Bridgett had continued: "So all of this has been building up into a very challenging discussion of: Where along the speciation time-line are we?" Scientists think about the formation of new species over a period of time. "For coyotes, this is happening in front of us, at a fast rate, and that is something we can observe and can measure and scientifically resolve. So a lot of people understand that time scale of research, but when we extend that time scale to wolves and coyotes and start asking questions about how long have they been a separate species—and that time frame seems to be very short, only a couple thousand years instead of millions of years—then we just snowball into a whole bunch of challenging issues."

I was confused. Didn't she just say they *weren't* separate species? No, wait, what she said was her *perspective* based on the evidence

---

[16] For some reason, I expected to be cutting through bone, but, duh, the tongue is a muscle.

she had been finding. Evidence leads someone to a conclusion, but that conclusion stirs up more questions; it generates new ideas and new hypotheses. Someone then goes and collects evidence that either supports it or refutes it or sometimes—often—doesn't give a clear answer either way.

Later Bridget wrote to me, *If you look at the behavior or ecology or morphology[17]—the red wolf is distinctly different from coyotes and gray wolves!*

So which of those aspects do we look at?

"Ultimately," Bridget concluded, "it means that canines are *really* unique and very hard to figure out with a simple, single study."

I thought research was supposed to help you cross questions *off* your list. Everywhere I looked, it was adding questions instead.

✖ ✖ ✖

I really should end this chapter right there on all that mind-blowing science, but I can't resist telling you just one more thing. Coyotes aren't the only ones bringing up questions about species. A bird's wing was found smooshed in the mud by a road on a treeless plain in Ethiopia. That wing from Nechisar National Park became mighty famous all around the world.

---

[17] *Morphology*: study of body shape, like the size of ears, length of snout, etc.

When they first found the wing, no one recognized it. It looked like it might have come from a type of nightjar,[18] but it was too big. Then scientists searched for a match by comparing it to every nightjar wing in the world that they could get data on,[19] but they came up empty-handed. Could it be a *new* kind of nightjar? Could you actually describe a new species from just 1 wing?

That started a worldwide frenzy. Telephones rang, papers were shuffled, emails zipped across the planet.

The experts said—drum roll please—"Yes!"

So all it took was 1 muddy roadkill wing to introduce us humans to an entirely new kind of animal. World of science, meet the Nechisar nightjar.[20]

Thank you, roadkill!

---

[18] Nightjars are nocturnal birds that hang out on the ground most of the time and look like a pile of dead leaves. Go camping in the eastern United States, and you may hear one kind of nightjar calling loudly, *"Whip-poor-will, whip-poor-will."* After about an hour of that, you won't care about poor Will or the beauty of the call, just about getting that bird to shut up so you can sleep.

[19] Guess where they found that data. You got it: museums. I can just imagine David grinning from ear to ear.

[20] Later on, some ornithologists spotted a living, breathing Nechisar nightjar, but I don't think they've caught one yet. Those birds are hide-and-seek champions!

CHAPTER 4
Roadkill Counts

Acountry song blasting, my wheels shredding the road... The road trip was fun until a curled opossum[1] caught my eye. I was pretty sure she wasn't playing dead. The red spot in my rearview mirror confirmed that.

One life. Extinguished. After seeing all the great stuff Melissa, Bridgett, and the others[2] were learning

---

[1] It was a North American opossum, *Dedelphis virginiana,* but conversationally we often call them "possums," which can get confusing because in Australia there's a whole different family of animals called possums. Common names can get confusing!

[2] Two scientists are looking for new medicines by swabbing out the mouths, noses, and "other" body openings of roadkill. Imagine how gunky those cotton swabs are! They found 4,000 different bacteria and may have struck gold—molecules from opossum ears seem to be effective in fighting a type of yeast found in human mouths.

from roadkill, I had grown a little callus on my heart that kept it from hurting too much.[3]

But ... what if she had babies?

I remembered this crazy, cute, heart-wrenching internet video of a pure white dog named Hantu, with what looked like a beanbag flopping around on his back. It was Poncho, a baby opossum. Hantu had adopted Poncho after his mother had been hit by a car. Opossums are marsupials—pouch and all—so if a mom gets hit, people look for babies. In Australia, pouch-pickers save tons of babies each year. Kangaroos or koalas, wallabies or wombats. People pull lucky little joeys from warm, dark pouches that could have turned into cold dark coffins.

I started to pull over to practice my pickpocket skills, but there was absolutely no shoulder—it was one of those rural roads where the pavement drops straight off into never-never land. Besides, school had just let out, so the road was crammed with cars.

Whose life was more important?

Three miles down the road, her face—pink nose, button eyes, and panda-like ears—began to haunt me.[4]

Really, I rationalized, if I had stopped and caused an accident, it wouldn't be just my life I was endangering.

But couldn't I at least do something?

---

[3] Not everyone likes opossums, but everyone should thank them. One study found that possums eat 96.5 percent of the ticks that crawl onto them. The scientists concluded that a single opossum may kill 5,000 ticks in a busy week! Now, imagine if opossums went bye-bye ...

[4] While still in their mom's pouch, baby opossums are pink, hairless, and helpless. Then they grow soft gray fuzz and adorable Yoda-like ears. All eight or so of them clamber out and up onto mom's back to go for a possum-back ride. Incredible fact: when in the pouch, they each bite and hold on to one of their mom's nipples, and their mouths fuse around it. If she's hit by a car, the nipples act like a crazy kind of seat belt, keeping her kids from being flung out of the pouch.

As I drove, a story about a teacher named Brewster Bartlett came to mind. The students at Pinkerton Academy had given him an interesting nickname: Dr. Splatt. One day he was driving home from a meeting about educational science projects. Other teachers were planning to have students count and record the number of monarch butterflies that successfully emerged from chrysalises. That sounded like a project for little kids. Dr. Splatt wanted something his ninth graders could sink their teeth into.

Then he saw an Unidentified Road Pizza (URP)—an animal too squashed to even tell what it was. What if ...

He called up the New Hampshire Fish and Game Department. They had people recording the number of deer, moose, and bear who didn't make it across the road, but the department didn't have the time, funds, or human power to deal with the rest.

What about the anoles, bluebirds, cougars, deer mice, and every other letter of the alphabet?[5]

Soon students were craning their heads out of bus windows, looking for roadkill, collecting data, and identifying dead bodies.

---

[5] Don't forget those URPs! They count too.

Over a 9-week period, Dr. Splatt and his students surveyed 70 miles of road and found 300 dead animals.

That, I thought as I pulled out onto a divided 2-lane highway, *is what I can do! Roadkill counts.*[6]

3/9/16, 2:25 p.m., Route 72, Eastbound Lane

Begin: Flint River Bridge

1 crushed possum

1 raccoon (by Flint River)

1 raccoon (by tributary to Flint River)

1 URP, light gray fur, fluffed, smattered, and scattered

1 raccoon

1 smudge with a tuft of gray tail waving in a
    truck's tailwind

1 coyote (by Paint Rock River)[7]

1 possum straddling the yellow line

1 URP on the verge[8]

1 possum? on the verge

1 URP on the verge

1 smudge on white line

1 tuft of hair and flap of skin on left verge

1 leg standing upright—armadillo?

1 large dark-and-white feathers by lake—osprey?
    Eagle?

1 possum

---

[6] Take it out of context and you could read that another way . . .

[7] Why so many by the river? Animals frequently travel along waterways. When a road intersects their path, they have to pop up and over the road to keep going.

[8] The "shoulder" or edge of the road.

1 squashed skunk on right verge
1 white thing, left verge
1 bird—vulture?
1 URP on center line
1 small black mound at intersection
1 tail
4 ducks all together on the bridge
End: Intersection with Highway 35 at Scottsboro

31.8 miles = 26 lives halted before their time

That is absurd, I thought. All that dying. It was too hard to think and drive, so I stopped recording, but I couldn't stop the questions from flooding in.

Why are all those animals hanging out on the road? Are all roads this dangerous? Is it just because it's spring? Why didn't they move out of the way? I wouldn't want to be a raccoon or possum around here. How many animals get hit each year? How did those drivers feel?

I knew I couldn't answer all those questions, but some answers had to be out there, so I dug into the research: book research, internet research, and people research. I started asking everyone I met to tell me their roadkill stories.[9]

---

[9] A school librarian told me about how her husband accidentally backed his truck over a turtle. Their daughter, who is in middle school, got serious about investigating it. She discovered its shell was made up of layers. Cool! I wonder how it grows.

My search uncovered some interesting answers.

How many animals *are* hit by vehicles? Depends on who you ask, where they looked, and what types of animals they counted.

In Tasmania, you'll find 1 carcass about every 3 kilometers. In Africa, the numbers can be more like 4.3 *every 1* kilometer. According-ing to the *Handbook of Road Ecology*, in the United States alone, there are some 2 million large mammals killed every year by vehicles.[10] Those same collisions injure 29,000 people and result in 200 human deaths.[11]

Yikes. I hadn't thought about people getting hurt. That's heavy stuff.

Maybe let's look at something we can maybe get a grip on. Some-thing little—insects.

One summer in Japan, a team of scientists collected dead insects from two roads every Wednesday afternoon (except when it was raining). Adding the totals from both roads and averaging them, they ended up with 5,004.3 insects killed per kilometer. Those scientists admitted that as hard as they worked to scrape up and count every little bugger, their results were probably a total underestimation—think of how many of the little guys stuck to the cars, got hauled off by ants, or were blasted far from the road by the whoosh of a tractor-trailer.

You see, no study is perfect.[12] They only counted animals on certain stretches of roads. What if they counted during the winter,

---

[10] Quoting the Humane Society, a Nat Geo explorer says it is more like millions of vertebrates *every week*. Once you're using that many zeros, it's all bad news.

[11] A moose could cause a pretty bad accident. Or a squirrel could, if a driver swerved to miss him. In Florida, the slimy remains of a single baby alligator caused a bicycle rider to lose control, resulting in a bike pileup injuring at least 6 people.

[12] Every scientific experiment has lots of variables to consider—other conditions that may vary and could alter the results. Paved versus unpaved. Urban or rural. Fast or slow traffic. What else might matter?

when certain animals move around less? And the animals can't raise their hand to say: "Present!" so surely some creatures get missed. Squished salamanders or snails don't catch the eye—or the media attention—like lions or rhinos do. Besides, dead bodies don't always hang around. One intrepid team staked out bloody bodies to find out how quickly they would disappear from the side of the road: 89 percent vanished within 24 hours.

So I never did figure out how many animals die from wildlife-vehicle collisions. Suffice it to say, it's a lot.

Another question: *Why* are animals hanging out on the road in the first place?

Guess what: reptiles like it. That big black surface soaks up all that warm sunlight. Scaly skin slides right on out there to cuddle up to a hunk of hot pavement. Especially in cool weather, ectothermic[13] creatures crave heat. Cold slows down chemical reactions, so cold muscles don't contract quickly. Before they're warmed up, snakes, turtles, and lizards literally can't get off the road fast enough.

Bighorn sheep get their kicks off the licks. That's right—they come to the road just so their big black tongues[14] can lick it. For them it's all about getting a salt supplement. You know how in the winter, the road crew spreads salt on the road to keep it from icing? Sheep and porcupine and deer and pronghorn and moose all like the salty sludge that washes off the road.

Along the interstate we've created fast food for armadillos. Wide, open areas, perfect for snuffling out underground bugs. If those run

---

[13] You might called them cold-blooded, but that's not fair. Their blood is not necessarily cold; it's the temperature of whatever they are surrounded by.

[14] Why's it black? I don't know! But you better believe I've sent that question to a bighorn sheep guy I know.

short, there's no shortage of dead bugs blown off windshields. Why go anywhere else?[15]

And let's not even start talking about all the other animals that come to the road for a main course of carrion—roadkill offers a buffet that keeps on giving.

Sometimes it has nothing to do with it being a road. Think of a porcupine. Even if he wants to scoot across, it takes time to shuffle across all 8 lanes of interstate.

My friend Mark told me about a monk parakeet that refused to leave the road. Imagine an 11-inch neon-green bird holding its ground as something like a dump truck barrels toward it. When a vehicle came too close, the bird would hop away but immediately fly back. Why? Its mate was on the road, lying lifeless on the asphalt.

Animals have lots of reasons to be on roads, but often, it's because they've got places to go.

Take a zebra chomping on some green grassy goodness. He suddenly realizes it isn't green or good anymore. When all his muzzle pulls up is dusty, dry, and brown, it's time to migrate. To find water and the best munchies, he and 200,000 of his closest friends[16] keep moving in a circuit across the Serengeti. Of course, his closest enemies tag along too—lions, leopards, cheetahs, and hyenas don't let their food get too far out of sight. If there's a road in the way, this crowd doesn't care.

In North America, the moose, elk, deer, and pronghorn hoof it when snow covers their food. In fact, some say the deadliest

---

[15] I'll tell you why. Because these possums on the half shell are perfectly adapted for suicide. Their secret defense against predators? Leaping 3 feet in the air. It scares off a coyote, but lands them smack-dab in the grill of a truck.

[16] Plus 500,000 gazelles and 1.5 million wildebeests. If they didn't move around, can you imagine the stench of their droppings?

animal in North America isn't a rattlesnake, grizzly bear, or mountain lion. It's a deer, no thanks to their size and frequent movement across roads.

In Manitoba, Canada, each spring, 75,000 garter snakes boil up out of limestone sinkholes. Some herpetologists and a few other snake-lovers stand right in that wriggling river of snakes. Hey, it's a perfect place to grab a ton of data.

Back in the fall those snakes had headed down, down, down into those living-room-sized underground spaces to escape the -40-degree-Fahrenheit winter.[17] Months later, they are all hissing with hunger. Up, up, up they push into the light and fresh air. After finding a mate, each snake has to boogie on out of there to find enough frogs to fill that empty tummy. Spreading out, the snakes have to dodge a few speeding tires.

Migration has its challenges.

When a road crosses an animal's path, the critter has got a choice: cross it or don't.

Roads result in habitat fragmentation—when an animal's playground is cut up into itty, bitty bits. Then there's no room for a big old animal like a mountain lion to stretch its legs. It's not just a "feel good" thing either. Habitat loss and fragmentation drive the decline of species.

Fortunately—or unfortunately—some species choose not to cross. Those animals live for another day, which is a good thing. However, when a road blocks their travel, they never make it to: water, food, their mother, a mate . . .

---

[17] There aren't too many of those perfectly cozy winter retreats, so the snakes travel up to 12 miles to claim their seats (probably on top of some other guy).

Imagine you are a fuzz-faced Samango monkey. You've got the important job of eating fruit and then spitting or pooping the seeds out, thus planting the trees of the future. A treacherous tar road stretches all along the base of your mountain. And for every road built, there are trees cut—and branches trimmed back to make room for tall vehicles—cutting off your leaf-lined route to the rest of the forest. You can hang out on that mountain, find a girl/boy-friend, have babies, and live there happily ever after. Life is good for you, but maybe not for your babies.

When a group of animals is trapped in the same place, they never mate outside of their little group. Their gene pool gets kind of stale. Isolation is not so good for the population. So a teenager[18] really needs to get outta there.

Many animals on roads are young guys looking for dates or gals looking for the best place to have a family.

Back to my list of questions. Maybe I'd do better with: Why are animals *hit*? How come they don't get out of the way?

The answers could go on and on.

All roads aren't created equal. All animals aren't created equal. All drivers aren't created equal.

There seem to be certain hot spots, places animals get hit more often. Curves, dips, and bridges create blind spots. When the driver and the animal can't see each other, it's bad news. So we should straighten out all the roads, right? To save all the animals? Not so fast. One Canadian study found that when you widen the roads and smooth out the curves, people drive faster. Higher speeds = more dead animals.

---

[18] Okay, not an actual "teenager," but a teenager in monkey or frog or panther years.

Sometimes.

Dr. Splatt and his students found the opposite: small, curvy, hilly roads—ones with slower speed limits—had higher roadkill counts. What gives? There are lots of variables to consider. Maybe we don't have enough studies yet to have an answer. Let's hope people keep collecting data!

After reading about hot spots, I started paying attention. On one road, I frequently noticed bodies in the same spot. It wasn't a blind spot, though. It was flat as a pancake, without a curve for a mile. Passing it a few more times, I realized something. Everywhere else along that stretch there's either a pasture, a field of crops, or a house on one side of the road or the other.

Now, there was plenty of forest in the area, but along that straightaway, it was like the "people stuff" had shoved the "nature stuff" back away from the road. Except in that one spot. On the right side, there was a ribbon of green running between two fields of yellow. A tunnel of trees snaking out from the forest in the distance. On the left side, one corner of a woodland met the road.

I wondered if this spot was where all the animals get hit because it's the only spot animals from the forest could approach the road without waltzing across a huge field or someone's front yard. Like it's their only hallway from the present to the future.

Of course, certain species seem to be asking to get hit. You know the type—deer in the headlights! Nocturnal[19] and crepuscular[20] animals have phenomenal adaptions for seeing in low light. For example, deer have slit-shaped pupils that can open much wider

---

[19] *Nocturnal*: active at night.
[20] *Crepuscular*: a cool-sounding word that means active at dusk and dawn.

than ours. This allows more light into the back of the eye where the sensory cells are. They also have a special membrane called the tapetum lucidum, which bounces light back over those sensory cells—it's a two-for-one deal! All great adaptations for seeing at dusk or at dawn. All reasons why, when headlights hit those night-adapted eyes, a deer is blinded like you are after a camera flash. Not being able to see, and not knowing what to do, the animal freezes.

If it were a wild cougar sneaking by, a frozen deer might just stay hidden long enough to see another sunrise. If, on the other hand, that cougar is of the four-wheeled persuasion, no more sunrises for Bambi.

Another reason critters get crunched is because of drivers distracted by texts, food, someone in the backseat . . . There are also people who go out of their way to hit snakes, jackals, and other animals they don't like—or maybe ones they like . . .

Apparently, some criminals like hyenas for their tails. An old tale tells that with the lift of their tails, hyenas can put their prey to sleep, making them easier to kill. Burglars burn a hyena's tail outside of a house, intending for the smoke to enter the house and put the owners to sleep, making them easier to rob. When you find a DOR hyena with a missing tail, it looks a little suspicious.

Right here in the US, a guy named Mark Rober put the scientific method to the test. Armed with a rubber turtle, snake, and tarantula plus a real leaf,[21] he put 1,000 drivers and 1 bicycle rider to the test. This guy found that 6 percent were "cold-blooded rubber

---

[21] The leaf was the "control." A control lets you see what happens if you didn't change any variables. Using a leaf as his control, Mark was testing if the rate at which people hit animals was any different from the rate they hit non-animal things on the road.

animal killers."[22] Of those, 6 percent hit the tarantula, 1.8 percent squashed the snake, and 1 percent smashed the turtle.

And are we just talking about automobiles here? One day, in the middle of my research, I unearthed an unbelievable photo of an elephant that had been run over by a train. An elephant! His hind legs sprawled out on chunky rocks, his skin sagged, his body disappeared under the train car. One tan line showed where the wheel crossed over his rib cage. My heart sank. It just wasn't right looking at the bottom of his soft gray feet.

Don't forget about planes, boats, bicycles,[23] skateboards, lawn mowers, and more! At this point in my quest, I was getting overwhelmed. I didn't want to go anywhere, afraid that even when I was walking, my foot might smoosh some miniature creature.

Why did I ever dive into roadkill? I wasn't sure I could keep going.

Roadkill is just. Too. Tragic.

---

[22] We should be fair and say Rober couldn't really know that they were aiming for the animals. Maybe they just weren't looking where they were going. Also, one theory says that when there is an object on the road, our eyes (and thus the steering wheel) are drawn toward it.

[23] Did I tell you about the flesh-colored goo I found in my treads one morning? ☹ So sorry, Mr. Earthworm.

CHAPTER 5

On the Trail of
Dead Devils

Beeee-Boooop, the digital tones of Skype greeted me, and the face of a dark-haired young scientist appeared on my screen.

It was Dr. Elizabeth Murchison, speaking to me from her no-nonsense office at the University of Cambridge. I had quit looking at roadkill. I thought I was done with it. But once you get a thing like roadkill in your head, you just can't stop seeing it. Or seeing references to it *everywhere*. That search engine in your mind just seeks it out all the time. So, these fascinating stories kept popping up, and sometimes I couldn't resist their call. After watching a video about Dr. Murchison's research on growling, screeching, sneezing Tasmanian devils,[1] I just *had* to talk to her. I scheduled an interview.

Elizabeth's not interested in Taz, the whirling cartoon character.

---

[1] Apparently, when devils disagree about who gets a tasty piece of rotting meat, they face off nose to nose, their ears flush, and they make a serious sneeze as a kind of bluff. Then, usually, somebody backs down and slinks off to find some other dead body.

It's real Tasmanian devils that float her boat. As in the scavenging marsupial that now survives in only one place on the planet—the island of Tasmania south of Australia.

Elizabeth started telling me about the roadkill discovery that changed her life: "I had been on this hiking trip with friends and family. It was over New Year's—which in Australia is in the middle of summer, obviously—so we had this *amazing* hike of . . . I think it was ten days out in wilderness. Basically, out there you just take a backpack and all your food and a tent and you are completely out there. It was an *amazing* feeling."

I'm thinking: That's my kind of trip—sign me up!

Right away I was charmed by Elizabeth's dialect. She'd grown up in Tasmania then lived in England for a while, so her speech was a really delightful blend. *Been* became *bean*. Instead of just *liking* something, she was *keen on* it. On top of that, she described everything as *amazing*. Then again, she was talking about rain forests off the southern tip of Australia. *Everything* there *would be* amazing.

She was driving through this beautiful gulley full of zigzags, a raging river, and ferns that tower over you like trees. It was in the middle of nowhere. She had told her mates about her scientific interest in Tasmanian devils, and that was when she spotted it.

"A devil, just there! We pulled over, and it was in fact a devil that had been killed by a car. And the amazing thing about this devil was that it had this tumor, which was the thing that was fascinating me at the time."

A tumor—hurrah! Wait, what?

A perfectly nice woman who calls a pink, lumpy tumor *amazing*? I had just met her, but Elizabeth didn't strike me as someone who was into animal cruelty. It made me lean in. It was just the kind of detail that told me how passionate she was about science. Just the thing to clue me in to how much I would like her.

Elizabeth had dumped all the gear out of her dirty backpack, wrapped the devil in a black plastic bag, and hauled it home to her parents' house. Her mother was thrilled.

"Most mothers—if their daughter brought home a squashed animal—would have been put off, but she knew I was really keen to work on this. So she was happy for me."

But why was Elizabeth keen to work on this dead devil? What was oh-so-exciting about a pink lump on its snout?

Later I looked at a picture of a devil with a tumor and it turned my stomach. This black animal—which looks like a bear cub crossed with a gerbil, but with honking big teeth—had the most grotesque glop hanging out of its mouth. Like a nightmare version of vegetable soup with red and pink and green and yellow lumpy things. Like vomit that wouldn't spill out of its mouth. It seemed like it was glued in place.

Elizabeth was keen on this sickening lump because she knew that people had been finding lots of Tasmanian devils with terrible tumors on their snouts. Elizabeth knew that the little lump of "devil facial tumor disease" was actually cancer. Elizabeth knew that the cancer was working fast to wipe out the species.[2]

This one little roadkill devil could be a gold mine for Elizabeth.

---

[2] Okay, okay, you fact-checkers: the cancer isn't the only thing killing these guys. There's also loss of habitat, natural predators, the fact that people once considered them pests and got paid to shoot them, and, of course, the ever-present predators—cars and trucks.

You might not realize it, but if you want to work on an endangered species, it's kind of hard to get your hands on an actual animal to study. And without a specimen to study, it's kind of hard for a scientist to get what she needs the most: data.

To get that specimen, first you have to find the critter. That isn't always easy when they're as rare as a Tasmanian devil.[3] Second, you need a permit, which can take months—even years—to obtain. Third, if you are a lowly graduate student like Elizabeth was, you are at the end of the line when people are passing out dead bodies.

So that little roadkill devil was kind of important to Elizabeth. He became the first Tasmanian devil from which she ever sequenced Tasmanian devil DNA.

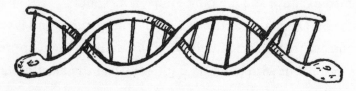

Remember, DNA is the secret code of life. Finding that road-killed devil was like finding a single tablet with internet access, when all the other devices in the world are hidden away deep, deep in the wilderness. Elizabeth had questions. There was a chance that the poor dead body could have answers.

Growing up in Tasmania, occasionally Elizabeth had gotten a glimpse of a devil in the wild. She loved that kind of thing. But by the time she was in grad school, those adorable little animals were disappearing. Experts were saying that in 20 to 30 years they would

---

[3] They are labeled "endangered" for a reason. Since 1996, when the tumor disease was discovered, in some areas 90 percent of the wild Tasmanian devil population has died.

be completely extinct from the wild.[4] You see, the disease that was first spotted in northeastern Tasmania was spreading across the country like a wildfire.

Before her roadkill find, Elizabeth had already come face-to-face with the disease. I had heard her tell that story on a TED Talk: "I remember the horror of seeing this little female devil with this huge, ulcerating"[5]—her nose scrunched as she said—"foul-smelling tumor inside her mouth that had actually cracked off her entire lower jaw. She hadn't eaten for days."

Elizabeth's brow furrowed. There was no hiding the sadness in her eyes. "Her guts were swimming with parasitic worms. Her body was riddled with secondary tumors[6], and yet she was still feeding three little baby Tasmanian devils in her pouch.[7] Of course, they died along with their mother."

Now, Elizabeth knew about cancer. She had knowledge on an all too personal level. When she was only 14 years old, she had to have a tumor cut out of her own body.

What Elizabeth didn't know—what scientists across the planet didn't know—was why the cancer was suddenly showing up

---

[4] Thankfully, some forward-thinking people have started raising devils in zoos and on islands, places that are protected from the disease. Maybe, just maybe, if we do lose all the wild ones, the cancer will kick the bucket for good and we could repopulate the wild with devils from those "insurance" populations.

[5] *Ulcerating*: festering, an open sore that won't heal.

[6] A primary tumor starts in one part of the body, and then pieces of it go floating through the body to begin growing in other parts. Those spots become secondary tumors.

[7] Yep, that's right. These mamas have pouches like kangaroos. A mama devil usually gives birth to 50 imps (baby devils) at a time. They run a mighty long race—all of 3 inches (7.6 cm)—to beat out their brothers and sisters to 1 of 4 teats tucked away in her deep, dark pouch. Four imps win first, second, third, and fourth place. The rest die. Ouch! I won't complain about getting a lousy old "participant" ribbon in my next 5K race.

everywhere. Killing devil after devil after devil—a really scary plotline for an animal that was already on the brink.

Some scientists had a hypothesis. They had some evidence about it actually being a virus; however, the facts didn't add up. Elizabeth had heard a rumor about another idea. . . .

To understand that rumor, I had to know a little more about cancer. I whipped out my phone and typed in "How cancer happens." Here's what I got from some colorful diagrams and text:

When a cell divides inside a body, the new cell gets a copy of the DNA from the original cell. DNA, the instructions about how a cell should behave, is sort of like a list of rules in a classroom. As the DNA is copied, mutations can happen. So a new cell might get two copies of part of the DNA or gets cheated and doesn't get a full copy[8]—or gets DNA that has damaged information.

Mutations aren't bad or good; they just are part of the process.[9] Usually, the cell doesn't even notice that a mutation has occurred. Occasionally, though, mutations instruct cells to do weirdo things. When a mutation tells the new cell to copy itself again + again + again + again + again + again + again + again + again, it can be a bad thing = a tumor. A growing lump of cells we call cancer.

That rumor that Elizabeth caught wind of? It was that this cancer in the Tasmanian devils was contagious.

Contagious? I thought. Contagious cancer doesn't make sense. Contagious cancer could be a very scary thing.

To me, it made sense that cancer can spread inside of one body.

---

[8] Like if you are out sick and have to copy a friend's list of vocabulary words, but you get distracted by a wicked new video game and skip some of the words.

[9] In fact, mutations that happen in reproductive cells are one reason every human on Earth doesn't look exactly the same. Thank goodness for them!

Cancer of the lip can end up in your hip. Cancer of the thigh might show up in your eye. But as terrible as cancer is, when it spreads in a body, it stays in that one body, right?

Normal cancer doesn't go leaping from one body to another.

Normal cancer kills itself. It spreads throughout the body until it kills its host. That is tragic. But what if it didn't kill its host? Could it keep spreading?

In Elizabeth's TED Talk, she described it a bit more clinically: "Given the right environment, the right nutrients, a cancer cell has the potential to go on growing forever. However, cancer... leads to the death of the cancer patient, and also to the death of the cancer itself. So cancer could be thought of as a strange, short-lived, self-destructive life-form. A dead end."

Except for this cancer.

To Elizabeth and other scientists, it looked like the devils' cancer could jump into new bodies. When the scientists dug into those tumors on the devils, they had noticed an odd thing. The DNA in the tumor cells didn't match the DNA from cells in the rest of the body. For example, a boy devil had DNA from a girl devil living in his face.

Looking closely, the scientists found that the DNA from tumor cells all around the country matched.

That was when it hit them. All the tumors in all those faces originally came from one tumor in one sorry devil. Somehow the cancer had escaped that animal's body and was hopping, skipping, and jumping through the devil population.

But how?

Then someone thought about what devils do when they meet each other. Occasionally it's a peaceful encounter, but if there's any food around, there's a lot of screaming, snarling of big toothy mouths, and snapping of jaws. Their jaws aren't little wimpy affairs, either. They're designed to crush bone.

I watched a video of one devil trying to mooch off another. The first guy (who became the defender) was chowing down on a tasty wombat carcass. The new guy had a clever tactic—go in butt first. That gave the defender a nasty choice: bite his butt or let him steal dinner. For a few minutes they pretended to work it out. Each gnawed on his own end of the wombat until . . .

Arrr. Aarrr! ARRRCH! The defender attacked. He chomped down on the other guy's face. No matter how much spinning or dancing the other kid did, the defender's jaws hung on.

Now, imagine if the defender had a mouth full of tumor. Little tumor cells would be swirling around in his spit. His bite might be like an injection, slow-acting but lethal, brimming with hyperactive tumor cells ready to implant into a new devil.

Man, I thought, that cancer has exactly what it needs. The right environment, the right nutrients, and the perfect delivery method right into a fresh, healthy body.

Those scientists were figuring things out.

Sitting there in my nice little safe home in northern Alabama with Piper thumping her tail by my side, I was kind of glad I wasn't out there in the field catching those cancer-spreading devils myself. *Who does that?* I wondered. Where did the scientists get the specimens they needed to figure all this out? Sitting there in her nice little office in Cambridge, England, Elizabeth told me: she has people mail her roadkill.[10] Think about it. You aren't going to go out and kill an endangered animal to study what's killing it.

---

[10] Imagine accidentally receiving *that* package! Note: Elizabeth also gets specimens who died from other causes.

Elizabeth isn't the only scientist using roadkill to save species. Amber Furness spent two summers driving a truck around at different speeds, watching dragonflies bounce off it. No, her goal wasn't to off the bugs; she wanted to determine the vehicle speed that killed endangered Hine's emerald dragonflies.[11] Turns out, the unlucky number is 30 miles per hour. If the truck was going slower, the insect was usually able to dodge it. Do you think folks would be okay going 29 miles per hour to save these insects?

Since 2009, the Brasilia Zoo has been freezing blood and other critical parts of roadkill anteaters and other rare species. Their plan? To one day clone[12] new animals out of those rescued roadkill pieces and parts.

And Dr. Michelle Stocker? Endangered species aren't rare enough for her. She uses roadkill to study extinct ones. You may have heard about her favorite little guys: dinosaurs. Imagine you are trying to put together a really big jigsaw puzzle and you don't even have the box with the picture on it. On top of that, some of the pieces are missing and you don't even know how many you're supposed to have. Kind of tough, right? That's not half as hard as it is to put together the bones of an extinct dinosaur, but it gives you an idea. To get a clue about what that final picture might look like, Michelle and her students go looking for roadkill.

You take a squashed salamander, plop it in an old salsa jar, cover it with water, and a *very tight* lid. Wait a few weeks. It gets all smushy, and rots. You pour off the nasty water—careful, Dr. Stocker warns; you don't want to splash it on your shirt—and voilà, you've got

---

[11] Time-out here. I'm *in love* with dragonflies. This is the only dragonfly on the endangered species list. I'm not sure if that's a good thing (i.e., there aren't many in danger) or a bad thing (no one cares enough to protect these beauties).

[12] *Clone*: to make an identical copy.

a skeleton puzzle. Now you try to put it back together. At least you kind of know what you are shooting for. Bonus: you should have all the pieces. That process trains your brain and your eye to understand how those kinds of bones should fit together. How to tell a right femur[13] from a left one.

Put yourself in Dr. Stocker's boots out in the barren rocks of the Devil's Playground, discovering a fossilized skull. If you were her, looking at that bone in the middle of nowhere, Arizona, what if you weren't sure how it connected to the neck? Or what portion of the bone might be missing? Or how the jaw muscles could attach? You think a few modern skeletons could help?

And that fossil Dr. Stocker found? Turns out it was so old, it was new. That's right. An ancient creature no one else had ever discovered. They named it: phytosaur![14]

So roadkill collections come in handy. "This way," Dr. Stocker says, "[those dead animals] are actually being used for science instead of whatever else could happen to them." What else *could* happen to them?

✖ ✖ ✖

Think way back to when Elizabeth Murchison hauled that one little roadkill devil into her parents' house. She had no idea that it would

---

[13] That big bone in your thigh.

[14] Think: A car-sized creature with meat-slicing teeth that looks like a crocodile loaded with extra armor and lived 220 million years ago. Phytosaur belonged to the archosaur group, which includes crocodilians, dinosaurs, birds, and lots of extinct critters.

launch her into a career of discoveries. Since then, she's started an entire lab called the Transmissible[15] Cancer Group. She's discovered a second kind of contagious cancer in Tasmanian devils. And she's spreading the word about this crazy cancer. Her personal mission? To beat the cancer and stop it from exterminating those spunky little critters that have become the mascot for her homeland.

And Elizabeth is just at the beginning of her career. Now she has more questions to ask. More discoveries to make. Right now she's asking: If cancer can spread in devils, can it spread in humans?

Now that's a big, scary, important question. Aren't you glad she's asking it? Aren't you grateful to that little devil who got Elizabeth curious?[16] [17]

After talking with Elizabeth, I was jazzed about studying road-kill again. Maybe my excitement for this sounds cruel, but you know what I mean. This stuff is *fascinating*! Think of all the good that could come from it—answers about dinosaurs, new knowledge about cancer, ways to save a species.

Elizabeth had talked as if scientists were always on the lookout for dead bodies. Is that true? What about other people? Who else might take advantage of that free resource?

---

[15] *Transmissible*: capable of being spread.

[16] Contagious cancer is probably very, very rare in humans. Dogs and soft-shelled clams, on the other hand, aren't so lucky.

[17] Way back in the 1950s, a gung ho scientist injected volunteer prisoners with syringes of cancer. Very few people did get cancer, but they were already ill, so their bodies might not have been able to fight it off like the rest of us. But stay on the safe side, and don't go around biting your friends—or your enemies!

CHAPTER 6

Please Pass the Salt

Early one morning my ringing phone got me out of bed. A red fox, my husband, Laddin, said, was dead on the side of the road not too far from our house. I almost jumped in the car in my pj's—I was in a race against the vultures, bacteria, and other cars—but then I thought better of it and got dressed. It was January, after all.

Would Dr. vonHoldt want a sample from a fox's tongue? Were there any graduate students who might need this body as a specimen? Does a museum need data from this fox? Questions pinged around in my head as I drove.

The red blotch on the pavement told me where to pull over.

She was gorgeous.

Fur so lush, so thick, so inviting that they should just put a swatch of it in the dictionary beside *luxurious*. She looked like a lady dressed in her finest: her body covered in a burnt-orange coat, her legs decorated in long black leggings, and her head capped by silky black-tipped ears.

She was grotesque.

A stalactite of blood hung from her nose. An inch of pink tongue protruded at an unnatural angle from her mouth and was punctured by her own clenched teeth. Congealed globs stood out like rubies on the white of her throat.

How had it happened? Why had she been on the road? Was she chasing something? Did she even see the car coming?

I wanted to know *her* story.

There were clues: the road, the blotch, the bloody stalactite. But not enough for nonfiction. I could guess that she was crossing the road just like I would or maybe there was some food on the shoulder that had drawn her in or maybe she was traveling down the road or maybe her kits were on the other side.[1]

I wanted to hear *her* tell *her* story.

Maybe one day I would piece it together, but I decided to at least not let her beautiful body go to waste.

You see, looking at all that roadkill year after year had changed my mind about something. In the past when I saw an animal stuffed and mounted, I was creeped out by it. Even the really nice mounts in a museum gave me the heebie-jeebies. But spending time with all those carcasses on the side of the road, I was struck by how much beauty was still there. And how much we could continue to learn from the actual skin and bones. So, shoving the heebie-jeebies aside, I had learned a new skill: taxidermy.

Way back when I worked at the McDowell Environmental

---

[1] One time, a biologist was awoken at 2 a.m. by odd calls in his backyard. His flashlight beam caught the eyes of a fox. The animal charged him. It bit his open palm. The scientist knew that was really weird behavior. The next morning on his way to work, he spotted a fox kit killed on the road. Had the late-night visitor been the mother? Was she mad? Mourning? Asking for help?

Center, there was a guy who used to turn roadkill into teaching materials. He'd skin them, flesh them, tan them, and voilà, we'd have beautiful furs and skulls. A science lesson on carnivores and herbivores is a whole lot better when you can poke your fingers through the eye sockets of a coyote or a deer.[2]

Remember that rattlesnake from Chapter 1? Dissecting it wasn't the end of that story. I kept that snakeskin for my own teaching. It had been easy, kind of like pulling off a really tight sock. But mammal pelts? Not so easy.

By the time this fox showed up, I had made lots of attempts at DIY taxidermy.[3] That Christmas I had even asked for a fleshing knife. I had bottles and boxes of tanning supplies squirreled away under my office chair, a shed for processing parts, a fenced enclosure to keep the bones safe while the flesh rotted away . . .

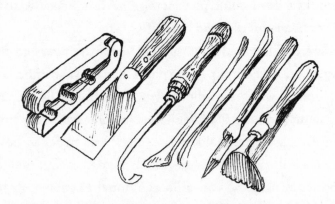

---

[2] Carnivores like coyotes have eyes in the front of their faces. That lets both eyes focus on the same object—extra-important for judging the distance to their prey. Herbivores like deer have eyes on the sides of their heads. If their eyes faced forward, they would mostly be staring at the grass in front of their face, not the coyote sneaking up beside them.

[3] This is another one of those things you should not try on your own. Just because an animal gets hit by a car does not mean it is a healthy animal. One other time I found a fox, as soon as I picked it up, three ticks crawled up my glove, aiming for my bare skin. Lyme disease, tick-borne relapsing fever, Rocky Mountain Spotted Fever—no, thank you. That fox didn't get to come home with me.

Hey, don't judge me. I didn't put the tail stripper, skiving knife, or membrane separator on that Christmas wish list.[4] For all those jobs, I just use a good old kitchen knife.

Warning: if things are getting a little too "Ewww" for you, you'd better just skip this chapter. For me to deal with it, I have to stop thinking about that pile of matter as an animal and start thinking of it as a carcass. It also helps to think "it" instead of "he" or "she."

Instead of letting that fox's body rot there on the side of the road or turning it in for the data, I decided to prepare the pelt. I hauled the carcass home. In a shed out back, I hung it upside down from its hind legs. I made an incision along the center of the abdomen (kind of like a zipper on a pair of jeans) and then along the underside of the tail and the insides of each rear leg.

After cutting a circle around each ankle,[5] I began the slow process of removing the skin. You know when you are trying to rip the wrapper off a piece of candy, but the candy has melted onto it? That's kind of what it was like. All of this connective tissue called fascia held it together like superglue. At some points, I had to use a blade to convince it to let go. It's important to get all the gunk off the skin, but you have to be very careful with the blade so you don't go poking holes in the hide.[6]

The carcass was pretty fresh, so it didn't smell too badly.

I sliced along, amazed at the lack of gushing blood. It was all

---

[4] Don't ask what all those things do—you really don't want to know.
[5] In a canine, the wrist and ankle are higher up the leg than you would think. Press your hand flat on a hard surface then raise up just your palm. See how your fingers stay down and your wrist is up in the air? Fox, wolves, coyotes, and dogs walk around on their finger and toe bones, called phalanges.
[6] Or your fingers. This is when I was really grateful for a husband who bought me gloves made out of that bulletproof stuff.

contained in streams of vessels, which joined to make rivers and led to the ocean of the heart. Then I came to the abdomen, and a mass of cranberry-colored goo and poopy smell spilled out. Oh. That car-strike caused internal bleeding. The intestines were all ropy. They made me glad I had forgotten to eat breakfast, because it surely wouldn't have stayed down with all that odor swallowing me whole.

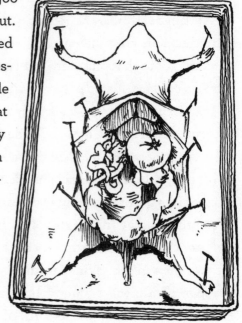

Finally, when my muscles were burning, fingers were good and sweaty, and guts had given up churning, I got to the most delicate part. As much as I wanted to rip the remaining skin off and just be done with it, I had to work inch by inch—no, centimeter by centimeter—no, millimeter by millimeter—to keep the ears, the nose, the lips intact.

There: I'd done it. The soft orange fur slipped down into a lump. *Thank you, Fox.*

My stomach growled, but I couldn't run inside for brunch. The longer the hide sat in a raw state, the more likely those little hairs would slip right out of the skin. Blame the bacteria. They attack the follicles[7] that hold the hair in. It was me against the bacterial clock. And the sun was creeping high in the sky.

---

[7] *Follicle*: small cavity or sac.

For the next stage, I put that fleshing knife to work cleaning up the hide. Watch out—the blade likes to snag and slice right through the hide. Better that than my thigh.

After an hour or so of scraping, I wiped the bloody bits from my blade, washed the skin in soapy water, rinsed well, and proclaimed it done. Well, that stage at least. Next, thank goodness, chemistry can do the hard work.

Please pass the salt.[8]

Yep, salt saves the day. Coating the fleshy side of the hide with a layer of non-iodized salt I reminded myself: *Don't skimp on it!* Salt draws the water out of the hide.[9] Without that water, decomposition comes to a screeching halt and keeps the stink at bay. After rubbing the gritty salt in, I laid the hide flat, and let it dry till crispy.

After I hauled the flesh and bones out to the old dog pen—where the flies and beetles could clean them up but the foxes couldn't carry them off—I went to have lunch. Whew!

Over lunch, let's talk more about the bones from roadkill. They've got value too. Sure, most people would leave them out there to get ground into the gravel, but not Francois Malherbe. No, that 11-year-old South African would pick them up,[10] take them home,

---

[8] Salt seems like such an everyday ingredient, but entire wars have been fought over salt. Every living being needs salt to make their cells go. Remember those ions we talked about in Chapter 1? Salt is full of that sodium ion. For over 8,000 years people have depended on salt to preserve food. (Do you like chips? Pickles? Jerky? All delicious because of—salt.)

[9] If you put a mixture full of ions on one side of a barrier and a mixture with fewer ions on the other side, and if water can move through that barrier to even out the concentration, it will. That is how salt draws the water out. Science nerds like me call it *osmosis*.

[10] Yep, where he lives, you can do that. Nope, he doesn't ever, ever kill anything; he just works with bodies in need of recycling. Mostly it's his dad who does the collecting. Safety first and all, you know.

and turn them into something important. He'd stick the body in water with dish soap and let it soak for 2 weeks, just like Dr. Stocker did with those salamanders in a salsa jar. When the flesh had all turned to mush, he'd pull the bones out and degrease them with ammonia and soak them again. Then, with a small pocketknife, he'd flick off any flesh that refused to let go. After bleaching the bones with peroxide, then drying them in the sun, they would be ready for the real work to begin.

You see, ever since Francois was 3, he's been fascinated with bones. Imagine a towheaded toddler who's crazy about musselcracker[11] jawbones! Nowadays he collects about 1 roadkill a month and turns it into a showpiece.

"We used to drive along the road and see something orange and think it was just a cat or a dog," Francois told me,[12] "but when you actually stop or look at it, it is a caracal or a bat-eared fox."

After spreading the bright white bones out on the family picnic table, Francois rebuilds the skeleton. He works on all the usual

---

[11] A type of fish that lives off the coast of South Africa.
[12] Francois lives 8,000 miles away from me, so I was pretty grateful for an app that let me visit with him for free. Thank you, internet!

animals—aardvark, grysbok, honey badgers[13]—well, usual for South Africa. He's run into a few problems along the way, like the fact that you can't go down to the local library and look up a book on which honey badger bones are toe bones or tailbones.

When he's got the bones lined up, Francois has got to hitch them all together. Out comes the superglue. He usually uses wooden rods to add stability, but when he rebuilt a giraffe—that's right, an entire giraffe[14]—he had to work a bit harder. He got his dad in on it, as well as his uncle, who's an engineer. That thing was big! His 6-foot-tall father could walk under its belly without ducking. Imagine trying to get it to stand up! Remember, it didn't have any muscles or ligaments or tendons to hold it together anymore. They ended up running steel tubes through the bones.[15]

After what can be months and months of work, Francois doesn't stick the skeleton in a closet. No, this kid has got his own museum space at a nearby zoo.

This is not all about making him famous. Francois does it because he likes learning how skeletons work. "I found out that there is a collarbone in some animals, but not all animals have it.[16] Only the ones that need to roll their arms have it. So animals that climb trees—um, primates. But a cat has got one called a flying collarbone, that is not a real collarbone, because it is not attached to any bone."

---

[13] Don't feel bad—I didn't know what any of these animals looked like either, but I checked out his online gallery and got to know their bones up close and personal.

[14] The giraffe was *not* roadkill, thank goodness. Can you imagine how scary *that* would be? When animals at a local wildlife reserve die of natural causes, the staff asks Francois to process the skeletons for them.

[15] In that hollow part where the marrow would be if the animal were alive.

[16] I don't *know* how he figured it out, but I picture him at that table digging and digging in a pile of aardvark bones till sunset, searching for a collarbone that just isn't there.

Cool! I love learning about this stuff.

He hasn't stopped there, though. Francois likes to share his story. He did a presentation to all the fourth, fifth, and six graders at his school. He's got a whole website to teach people about it. He's even been on national TV! When Francois saw how many bat-eared foxes were DOR in a national park, he got brave, wrote an article, then submitted it to a conservation organization. His newsletter article has been read by people all over the world.[17]

And, I reminded myself, he was just a little kid when he started it all.

✗ ✗ ✗

Back to the red fox skin. After it dries for 24 hours or so, it is time to pickle the hide. Please pass the salt—again. First, we mix the salt with acidic crystals and lots of water. You know about acids and bases, right? Acid like you find in lemon juice stings chapped lips. Acid like you find in batteries burns skin right off the bones. These crystals are somewhere in between. We drop the hide in and let it brew for several days. Anytime you get a hankering to, you can pull the drippy skin out and put that fleshing knife to work some more. Me, personally, I was tired of that.

Since we used an acid for the pickling, we need a base to stop the process. Sodium bicarbonate (better known as baking soda) does the job quite well.[18] You know those little pH tests you do in science class? The ones where you use strips of colored paper to indicate the 0-to-14 scale? Those come in real handy here.

---

[17] It's how I found out about this amazing young man and am able to share his story with you.
[18] To get rid of the bucket of acid, I dumped boxes of baking soda in, not bothering to measure. Oops! Bubbles rose right out of bucket, spewing nasty water all over the place.

You thought we were done? Not so quick. Now we finally get to tan the hide. We could go gather acorns, wait for them to boil, and use the acid leached out of them. Or we could use the animal's brain.[19] Me, I just crack open the bag of powder from the tanning supply store, pour it in with—guess what—more salt, and let it sit for another day or so.

Finally, finally, finally we've got a tanned hide.

But it's as hard as stiff plastic.

Ever heard stories of people who chewed leather to "break" the hide? You go right ahead. I'll just use leather oil and elbow grease.[20] The goopy oil soaks into the skin as I work it back and forth and back and forth and back and forth over the rounded end of a board. I last for just about 20 minutes. After 3 days of doing that several times a day, we've got a gorgeous, soft rust-orange fox pelt. Rubbed against your cheek, it feels like the cushiest coat you ever had.

Before this, I never understood why people would want to wear an animal's fur. Now I

---

[19] Yep, brains work. No one completely understands how, but basically squished-up brains are full of fat and a phospholipid called lecithin. Phospholipids have the amazing ability to bring oil and water together. The lecithin may help the skin suck up the fats from the brains, thus making the skin soft and "tanned."

[20] Basically the oil replaces the water that was in the skin, preventing it from rotting and also making it nice and soft. Ahhh.

get it, but I still don't want to wear it. I had a different purpose in mind. I slipped the fur over my arm like a puppet. For a moment I did the puppet thing, trying to bring her back to life. But I *still* didn't know her story. And without a story, a puppet's just an empty sock.

Remember that vet student who said, "Roadkill—it's not the end of the story"? I still didn't have the full story, but somehow I felt like I was finding bits and pieces—a femur here, a jawbone there. Perhaps, somewhere down the road, they'd fit together like a red fox skeleton.[21]

---

[21] In case you were wondering, after the beetles and friends were done with the fox's bones, I fished them all out of the dirt and tried to puzzle them back together again.

CHAPTER 7

Rogue Taxidermy

Track the search term *roadkill* for two years like I did, and you'll turn up some really crazy stuff on the internet. Is this stuff even real? A roadkill bingo T-shirt,[1] a company that turned a dead badger into a submarine drone (with water jetting out of its backside), and a most inappropriate Halloween costume. One thing that kept popping up in my results was *rogue taxidermy*.

Rogue taxidermy? What's that?

To borrow the words of the Minnesota Association of Rogue Taxidermists, rogue taxidermy is "a genre of pop-surrealist art[2] characterized by mixed-media sculptures containing conventional taxidermy materials that are used in an unconventional manner." Translation: they turn pieces and parts of dead animals into "art." Search for images, and you'll get pics of:

---

[1] What would your folks say if you took that on your next family vacation?
[2] Also called *lowbrow*, this kind of art often uses a comic approach, references to popular culture, and sarcasm to present the world in a new way.

- a Foosball table where the players are actual squirrels and other dead rodents
- a mishmash creature with a bird's head, a turtle's shell, and a squirrel's tail
- a mouse dressed up with a white satin bow, being sold as a Mother's Day gift

Something about those just didn't sit right with my more traditional (read: old-fashioned) idea of art. Was this a morbid[3] pastime to make fun of dead animals? Innocent creatures who had lost their lives? And where—I wanted to know—were they getting those animal skins? Did they *kill the animals*?

These questions took me all the way to New York City. There, among the Statue of Liberty, 89 museums, 6,000 miles of roads, and 8.5 million people, I found someone with answers: Amber Maykut.

To be honest, I was pretty uneasy as I headed toward her second-story art studio.

From her website I'd gathered that Amber was a twentysomething, tattoo-covered hipster who claimed her art was made from roadkill. Well, that sounded better than killing off a cute cuddly creature for art supplies, but a quick scan of Etsy clued me in that some rogue taxidermists made good money selling their creations. What were they doing? Turning an animal's tragedy into a tidy profit?

With those thoughts boiling around in my brain, I climbed the stairs to the interview. *I'm going to try to have an open mind,* I told myself.

---

[3] *Morbid*: an unhealthy interest in death.

Within minutes of stepping into Amber Maykut's studio, I realized it was also her home. Blond and beautiful, Amber lived surrounded by dead animals. Creepy? Kind of, but they were also exquisite.

It's obvious that Amber is a passionate person. "Just yesterday," she gushed, "I taught a private taxidermy lesson to a high school girl who was here on vacation from New Orleans. She was *so excited*." Amber sounded as thrilled as students spilling out the door on the last day of school. Sometimes kids as young as 7 show up for her class. "They have so many questions and they are so inquisitive and they are, like, incredibly fascinated by it."

Hey, that sounds like me!

"How else or when else would you get to touch a squirrel and know what its fur feels like? Especially here in New York City. Or how coarse a skunk's fur can be. You would never touch a live skunk, you know."

"I've never touched a live skunk," I told her. "I've never touched a dead skunk." Or wanted to before that moment, but Amber made me want to. "So, what's a skunk feel like?"

"It's really greasy."

Skunks, bears, and pigs are all so fatty, you have to use a degreaser to clean up their fur.[4] I'm one of those oddballs who doesn't mind smelling a skunk, but thinking of holding an incredibly stinky skunk in my hand, trying to skin it? My face must have shown what I was thinking, because Amber went on to explain that the smell comes from an oil held in a sac: "As long as you don't burst that scent sac, then it is fine."

She jumped up and opened her freezer.[5] "I have one right here."

Her kitchen was neat; so neat, I wondered if she had scrubbed it just for my visit. The white counters and stove sparkled. Her freezer was full but orderly. Lumpy plastic bags were stacked right on top of the ice-cube trays. I glanced down at the ice cubes in the cup of water Amber had given me.

What else might be floating in there?[6]

---

[4] I had tried to skin a raccoon once. They are so slimy with oil, you can hardly keep ahold of the skin when you are trying to wrench it from the body. Your gunky hand keeps slipping right off the skin and flying into your chest. And then when you finally, finally succeed, you are left with this greasy rag of a fur that won't dry off no matter how many paper towels you use. That's how I learned about picking the right time of year to skin things. In the fall their fur is getting nice and thick, but so are their fat reserves. I also discovered that dish soap cuts raccoon grease just as well as it cuts bacon grease ☺.

[5] Yep, another freezer—the second most common place you find roadkill.

[6] Do you realize that tiny molecules from every item around you are drifting in the air? Inhale, and some get sucked up to the smell receptors in your nose. When I'm smelling brownies baking, that idea doesn't bother me, but rotten flesh? Suddenly I wasn't thirsty anymore.

Not finding the skunk, Amber whisked a squirrel skin from a bag. "So you can see," she raced on, "he's got some road rash on him from whatever he's been through. And then his little hand came off." Her lips pouted.

Oh.

The hand, like the rest of the skin, had already been tanned and was turned inside out. It looked like a wad of used gum. "That came off in the accident and somebody recovered it?" I asked.

Amber had. I imagined her, searching the gravel at the side of the road. That takes dedication. She went on to explain that much of the clothing or humanlike poses she uses—the anthropomorphic taxidermy—often serve as a bandage to cover up the damage.

Sometimes an injury acts as inspiration. "Like this is . . ." Amber held up the little squirrel's face, showing me how one side was scraped raw. "Okay, he is going to need an eye patch—maybe he's a pirate. Maybe he can be the Phantom of the Opera, or Zorro." She swished one arm in a sword-fighter motion, tucking the arm with the missing hand behind his back.

My mind scrolled through the internet pics that I had assumed were making fun of the animals. Could those rogue taxidermists have been applying "bandages" too?

Then we moved to a corner lined with shelves above a work desk. Racks on a pegboard were filled with screwdrivers, a row of pointy metal things, four types of tape, and trays of scissors. A whole slew of colorful prize ribbons got us talking about Amy Ritchie-Carter, a gal who fell in love with taxidermy at the age of 13, using roadkill her dad found on his early morning paper carrier route. By 15, Amy had won a ribbon at the National Taxidermists Association Competition. Wow!

There's such a thing as a *national* taxidermists competition? And teens can compete in it? Sure. Amber rattled off a list of taxidermy contests I should go to.

Then she held up a cream-colored form that was the shape of a squirrel. She added a tiny orange ball to its outstretched arm. "I was thinking of making him a basketball player." She cocked her head, studying the shape. "Carve it down. Tuck these in." She was pointing to some part I couldn't see, but I didn't want to interrupt—I could almost see the gears turning in her mind. "Then test the form. If it's too small, I build it up with clay. It doesn't have to be all ... so ... sad."

A squirrel basketball player. That *could* come off like it was making fun of the animal, or it *could* be seen as reusing a skin that would have sat on the road and attracted more animals to become victims themselves.

And come to think about it, fur is full of protein.[7] That protein had to come from the nuts the squirrel ate. And those had to come from the tree that sucked the nutrients right out of the air and the ground. To get her art supplies, Amber was recycling those. To get most art supplies, we cut down trees to make paper. We dig up minerals from the

---

[7] The protein is called keratin. Yep, the same one in your hair and fingernails.

ground to make pigments. Why not reuse the ones already lying around?

Huh.

Four dark brown hooves sat on her desk, forming the square base of a lamp. Short brown fur covered the legs, which stretched up to the metal fixture. I couldn't resist touching it. Now, looking at the plastic lamp sitting on my desk, I'm feeling kind of envious, kind of guilty.

The deer legs weren't from roadkill. Amber also recycles stuff from the butcher, the fur industry...even her friends' pet food.[8] She used a freeze-drying machine—the kind used to make astronaut ice cream—to wick away the moisture and keep the deer legs from getting stinky.

Amber dug a furry skin out of a crinkly grocery bag and held it over the kitchen table. It was the skunk she had been looking for earlier. There wasn't even a hint of skunkiness to it. I leaned in to get a better look at a paw. Five blue-gray nails, each as long as Amber's thumbnail, glistened. Tidy and clean, as if they had just had a manicure, the nails reached out from jet-black fur. They were a haunting color. If an artist tried to re-create that, could they ever succeed?

---

[8] You know how people feed their pet snakes frozen mice? Well, snakes don't need the fur. Amber strips it off before the snakes are fed. For us, it's like peeling an orange before we eat it.

The fur was solid black, lush, and dense. My instinct was to pick it up and rub it on my cheek, but it was actually kind of coarse.

"How do you find the roadkill?" I asked.

"I remember when I was first getting started on taxidermy, I was like, 'I really wanna do some taxidermy. I really wanna find some roadkill. When will I ever see some?' And now it's like I am a magnet for it. I am like 'that girl.'" She made air quotes. "My phone is blowing up with *I just saw a dead animal. Thinking of you.*"

My mind flashed to roadkill pics friends had sent to my phone:

> A whippoorwill with mysterious blue feathers in
>   his crop[9]
> The hollowed-out eyes sockets of a beaver,
>   squirming with maggots
> A pond slider[10] that Laddin rescued from the road

"People get it in their minds that it's like a bloodbath. Like you are going crazy with the guts and everything. But it's not a murder scene." Amber looked up, right into my eyes. "The way I do taxidermy is, I freeze the animal first. I use a scalpel to remove the carcass from the skin. It feels like an ice cube. It's like taking the skin off a chicken."

We had moved back to the comfy chairs in her living room. Her black cat was rubbing against my legs. Amber was telling me how great it was to send bones off to the dermestid beetle colony instead

---

[9] Birds don't have pockets, so when food is plentiful, they may gulp an extra serving. Some birds have a crop—an expanded pouch in their throat—where they store the food until they are ready to digest it.

[10] A type of turtle.

of having to boil, bleach, and scrub them with a toothbrush. Tell me about it.[11]

"What is your favorite part of the process?"

"Bringing it back to life. Building it up. Giving it a second life. You know, I was trying to think of a name for my business, and I was thinking of something like: Death Is Not the End."[12]

Amber was figuring out a way to let these animals tell a story, and that's pretty amazing if you ask me.

---

[11] Once, before I knew better, I tried cooking the meat off bobcat bones—in a hotel microwave. *Not* a good idea. Stinky! I feel sorry for the next guy who tried to nuke a bag of popcorn in there.

[12] FYI, Amber decided on the less ambiguous name—Brooklyn Taxidermy—and her business is flourishing!

CHAPTER 8

Oh Deer!

Something Amber had said gave me an idea. She knew of a zoo that fed roadkill to their animals. Really? That seemed pretty ingenious. Was it true? Did other places do that?

One day, when I was down on the Gulf Coast playing tourist with friends, I found some answers.

Standing atop a wooden platform overlooking a swamp, squished in a crowd of people, we watched a man pull a blue ice chest past a shape that reminded me of cement lawn art. The shape was sprawled out on neatly clipped grass: 4 clawed paws, a 6-foot tubular body, and a spiked tail with its tip dropping off the bank into a swampy river. A ripple in the murky water stole my attention. A bump, 2 eyes, a snout—and suddenly a second alligator rose from the depths and marched, robot-like, toward the man. Then a third. A fourth.

Trapped! The man was caught between the gators and a 6-foot fence. They formed a semicircle around him. He didn't run. Didn't try to leap the fence. Instead he released the handle of the ice chest and stepped toward one of the gators.

I jumped as a voice boomed over the loudspeaker. "How is everybody doing this morning?"

It was chow time at Alligator Alley.

"Haven't lost anybody yet, have we?" The voice boomed again. I noticed a second, younger man wearing a microphone headset. "My name is Joseph, and this is my main man, Tater. Go ahead and ring the dinner bell." He motioned to his daredevil partner.

Thump, thump, thump. Tater drummed on the ice chest.

Four more gators slid out of the palm-fronded jungle on the opposite bank. Two others lumbered in from the left, and still more plowed in from the water on the right, looking like oversized dogs eager to retrieve a stick. They all streamed toward Tater . . . No, they were heading for the ice chest!

"Currently, inside the swamp we have a little over 200 alligators—204 to be exact." Joseph opened the ice chest and pulled out a fist-sized chunk of pink flesh. The crowd around me leaned forward.

Joseph explained that these alligators used to live in the wild but had been labeled "nuisance animals."[1]

He tossed the chunk into an awaiting mouth.

"Oooooh," went the crowd.

"Basically, what landed them here, though, is just being an alligator. What used to be creeks and swamps and bayous has now been

---

[1] Wild animals are labeled "nuisance animals" when they are someplace or are doing something that people don't like. Sometimes, if they're lucky, like these guys, there's a wildlife sanctuary to take them in. Other times, they are—um—eliminated.

turned into waterfront property. So just being a gator is what got some of these guys in trouble."

A few, though, had also done a little something extra to put themselves in the doghouse. Captain Crunch, who hailed from Lake Seminole, Florida, had been in the habit of crawling out of his lake and swallowing 4-legged snacks of the canine kind. Pet owners were none too happy about that. But really, what's a gator to do? His hunting grounds *had* been taken over by manicured lawns and little Fidos.[2]

For 15 minutes, Joseph and Tater tossed hunks of meat to the animals. The gators chomped, swallowed, and opened up for more.[3] Joseph let us know that they weren't attempting to fill the gators up. Each animal could eat 1/5 of its body weight. "Prince Eric, the biggest one hanging around today, I'd put him at 600, maybe 700 pounds," he said.

After doing the mental math, I told my friend, "That's a lot of food. Wonder where they get all that meat?" I had a sneaking

---

[2] Captain Crunch's stats: length—13'2"; weight—over 800 pounds. He holds the official world record for American Alligator Bite Force: 2,980 pounds.

[3] Gators don't chew. Those 80 or so teeth? They're designed to puncture hides, break bones, and sheer tendons. A 10-foot gator can have a bite force of 2,000 pounds. Joseph said our bones start snapping at around 450.

suspicion, so after the show I went up and asked Joseph who all those hunks of flesh used to belong to.

"Deer—big deer."

"Is it ever roadkill?"

"Yeah, the sheriff's been calling me here lately."

I never thought about it, but getting rid of roadkill could be a big job, especially in the fall, when deer are in rut[4] and collide with vehicles pretty often. Usually, it's the sheriff's—or in some places, the road department's or the health department's—job to get rid of roadkill. The zoo Amber had mentioned? The New Jersey Department of Transportation actually pays them to gather the roadkill. And the 11-year-old who's part of that family business? He helps too.[5]

Using roadkill this way seems like a no-brainer to me. Normally the state would have to pay an employee to schlep it somewhere, and where are they going to take it, anyway?

Turns out, lots of roadkill ends up in the landfill.[6] But when there's an outbreak of some disease, like chronic wasting disease,[7] you can't even throw the carcasses away. The New York State Department of Transportation came up with a creative

---

[4] *Rut*: the mating season for deer. With one thing on their mind—girls, girls, girls—the bucks kind of forget that "Look both ways" rule.

[5] One year, the zoo got paid about $25 per deer. Think of all the money they saved on lion chow!

[6] *Landfill*: dump.

[7] Chronic wasting disease (CWD) is found in elk, moose, deer, etc. and caused by a prion—a protein gone bad. The prions attack the central nervous system (brain and spinal cord) and sometimes spread to the peripheral nervous system (everything else: nerves that let you see and pee). As you might guess from the name, deer with CWD waste away—they lose weight—and might also grind their teeth, walk in repetitive patterns, and drool—none of which are good survival strategies. If a body gets chunked into the landfill, it might never rot. Nobody wants a mummified body full of prions sitting around for thousands of years, so in areas where CWD is present, landfills close their doors to deer carcasses.

solution—compost! Seriously. They've got over 25,000 animal bodies to deal with every year.[8] So they take a load of wood chips (from all the trees they trim along roads), dump it down, lay out 3 or 4 deer bodies on top of the pile, and cover it all with another dump of wood chips. The next day, they start all over again.

Thanks, bacteria! They gobble up all that yummy goodness.

I visited one of those compost yards. You'd think the place would reek, but it smelled like fresh mulch. I plunged my arm into one of those piles (one that was completely "cooked"), and it was just . . . dirt.

The decomposition process heats the pile up to 150 degrees Fahrenheit, killing off the bad germs.[9] The only thing that's left is clean dirt—it comes out cleaner than the wood chips that went in—and a few random tough parts like hip bones and teeth. The department of transportation then uses that clean, rich dirt for all their landscaping needs.

Brilliant!

It's called the cycle of life.

Similarly, I think, gators eating deer is just nature doing its thing. In a way, Alligator Alley was not only helping out those gators with no other place to call home, they were helping out their county by getting rid of unclaimed bodies. Pretty nifty.

---

[8] In Ulster County alone, they get 700–1,000 deer a year. One guy picked up 7 in one day!

[9] The magic of compost happens when you mix organic matter (read: anything that has been alive), water, oxygen, and bacteria. In the organic matter, you have to have a balance of carbon and nitrogen. Wood chips are made from carbon dioxide pulled right out of the air by leaves. Deer muscles are made of protein; protein is made of amino acids; amino acids contain nitrogen. Too much carbon, and the pathogens (the bad guys, like E. coli, that make you sick) take over. Too much nitrogen, and it'll stink of ammonia. Too little oxygen, and it'll smell like rotten eggs. When the mix is just right, the good bacteria get working and produce heat. That heat kills off pathogens.

Believe it or not, alligators, zoo animals, and bacteria aren't the only ones eating roadkill.

People do too.

"If you hit it, you should eat it."

Wait, *what?*

During a phone call early in my quest to learn about roadkill, Fraser Shilling had made that shocking statement. At the time, it seemed pretty outrageous. I almost didn't even write it down. Was this guy for real? I had never met him. All I knew about him was from what I'd read on the internet. Was he really encouraging people to go pick up rotted meat and eat it?

Eventually, I met Dr. Shilling in Salt Lake City at the International Conference on Ecology and Transportation. As a road ecologist,[10] he had trekked from his home state of California to Salt Lake City to meet with 400 other folks from across the globe who all wanted to talk about roadkill. Think of it: 400 *professionals* whose job it was to prevent roadkill.

Turns out, Fraser's not the only one talking about eating roadkill. In states such as Minnesota, Montana, and Michigan, there are laws that encourage people to pick up dead deer and turn them into summer sausage or pepperoni sticks. In 2016, Washington State passed a bill allowing people to salvage road-killed game as long as they had a permit. In the first 6 months, 949 deer and 112 elk were picked up for dinner. If an average deer weighs 130 pounds and then

---

[10] How cool is that? Road ecology is a new branch of science with its own 500-page textbook and everything. It's not just about roadkill, though. There are some positive aspects, like how wildflowers along roads can help bees and butterflies, how a population of Canadian coyotes has learned to cross roads at midnight to avoid cars, how some spotted salamanders have adapted to the new salty conditions caused by runoff from roads, and how roads can be built to save animal lives.

you take out the hide, bone, blood, and guts, you get around 50 pounds of meat. That's 200 burgers' worth of free meat!

But "free" isn't the only reason people eat roadkill. When her husband hit a roadkill deer at midnight, Crystal Sands knew she couldn't go to bed.

"For me, it seemed like it would be wrong to waste it," Crystal, a young mom who lives in Maine, said. "We had made the decision to try to farm a little bit. We had chickens, and I was going through the process of what I consider 'putting my money where my mouth is.' If I am going to eat meat, then I should try as much as I can to eat meat when I know where it comes from. I know it has had a decent life; I know it has been treated well."

But she had never dealt with a dead deer before, so, hello, YouTube! Crystal admitted that she let her husband do the "processing"[11]—she was just too soft-hearted to do it herself.

The whole incident had been pretty intense for her. "It was more profound than sad...I had never touched a deer. To feel its fur and its nose and eyes and everything." Her face went kind of cloudy, and a soft smile spread. "I thought I might be crying and devastated—and I did cry—but I studied it more than I thought I would.

"Even though it was a small deer, it was so big and so strong and so, so magnificent. I looked at its hooves and legs, and everything seemed so *strong* and beautiful."

She came away from the experience thinking that everyone who eats meat should process an animal once in their life. That would

---

[11] To process a deer: 1. field-dress it (dig out the slippery, slimy guts—where the germies hang out); 2. skin it (keeping the hair away from the meat, peel the skin back from the meat with a really sharp knife); 3. quarter it (take the legs off at the joints and hack off the main hunks like tenderloin, brisket, ribs); and 4. trim it (slice down a big ham into roasts, steaks, or whatever).

give people an "understanding that meat is from an animal, a life, a being. It is not just a package you get from a grocery store.

"I really understand hunters so much more now."

Crystal's 6-year-old son, Ronan, had missed out on the butchering, but the next morning he happened upon the carcass hanging in their cold room. "I was like, 'What the heck?'" he said.

When I asked Ronan about eating the venison,[12] he said, "I expected it to be like most meat, which is kind of blah and icky." He puffed up his chest and added, "I only ate it with ketchup."

Okay, eating a deer that you just hit, I get that. It's not really much different than eating one you shoot—other than, of course, the cost. After getting the repair

bill for his truck, Crystal's husband had made a sour joke about what an expensive steak that had been. A typical deer-vehicle collision costs around $4,000.[13]

But, it's harder to swallow that people eat dead animals they find

---

[12] *Venison*: what you call deer meat when you eat it. When you eat a burger, you don't say "I'm eating cow"; you say, "I'm eating beef." I wonder if people created that other word to avoid feeling like they were eating an animal.

[13] Okay, my hunter friends, I know that ammunition and rifles (or bows) and licenses and deer stands and camo clothing are all expensive, but I hope you get more than one kill off all that!

just lying around on the road. Over in England, there's this man, Arthur Boyt, who says he has been tucking into roadkill since he was 13 years old. He eats roadkill—other people's roadkill—on a regular basis. He's 77. I guess it hasn't killed him. I had read online articles about how he finds his supper along the road.[14] As you can imagine, this bloke's got quite a reputation. I watched an online video of him—*viewer discretion required*—and some parts seemed logical, but other parts were kind of outrageous. Let me make this clear: I am *not* recommending you copy this gentleman. *I'm* not copycatting this gentleman. But I *was* fascinated.

So I tried to find him. Could I go visit him? Would I be brave enough to eat what he ate? I couldn't find a phone number or an address or an email for him anywhere. I resigned myself to being satisfied with the online information.

In the video, Mr. Boyt is wearing black gloves decorated with images of finger bones, an oversized red wool sweater, and a cute baby blue knitted cap; he looks like anyone's granddad. He's a taxidermist who decided to eat the bodies instead of throw them away. He's swallowed all kinds of stuff: polecats,[15] bats, swans,[16] hedgehogs, rats, and even a whale.[17]

---

[14] This gives "to-go" orders a whole new meaning!
[15] A European polecat is a relative of the skunk—both have stinky oil glands.
[16] Tastes like mud.
[17] Did the whale run into a boat?

He's standing on the white line, cars whizzing behind him. He reaches for a badger. "Well, it's not been squashed. Hmm...I would say it's been here for probably at least a month. But it's been very cold weather, so it has kept. It's edible, I reckon." He carries it home.

"I've been ill from eating food from a buffet," he says, "but I've never ever been ill from eating roadkill. If it is well cooked, I think there is very little chance of any bugs or bacteria surviving."[18]

Later, he plucks curled carcasses out of his freezer.

"This is my favorite here." He points to pink muscles on the hand-sized skull of a badger. Stripped of fur, the head glistens with ice crystals. Four canine teeth stand like corner posts in a fence of teeth. "You've got the big muscles here, and you've got the salivary glands, you got the tongue, you got the eyeballs (very essential for good eyesight),[19] and then you've got the brain." He jabs his finger toward the hole in the back of the skull.

"So you've got 1, 2, 3, 4, 5 different tastes and textures in one saucepan. They all taste different"—his tongue waggles out of his mouth—"and feel different."

I can't get over how fascinated I am by this man and his choices. A year later, I'm still curious, still not satisfied with just a video and words on a screen. I scour the internet for some scrap of information to help me locate him. I send messages to every Arthur Boyt I can find on social media. I latch on to the idea of using his hometown to narrow the search, and run search after search. Then I find

---

[18] Maybe that's true, but I'm sure not gobbling down any roadkill armadillo. They can carry Hansen's disease. You might know it as leprosy. According to the chief of the National Hansen's Disease Program, researchers first confirmed the spread of leprosy into Louisiana armadillo populations by sampling roadkill. No need to panic. Just don't go touching or eating armadillos!

[19] Is he talking about the badger's sight or that eating it will help you with your eyesight?

a letter posted to the internet and written by one Arthur Boyt. But is it *my* Arthur Boyt? It is a formal letter in opposition to plans to install a wind farm. It's written by someone who has conducted over 200 surveys of birds—packed with observations of local birds that could be impacted by the proposed wind farm—and who uses data collected from roadkill.

Bingo! *And* the letter includes a return address. I scribble out a letter to Mr. Boyt and run it to the post office. Then I wait and wait and wait for it to make its way across the ocean. Weeks later, Laddin and I puzzle over a blue envelope that shows up in our mailbox. It had been so long, I'd forgotten to expect it, but a queen's head on the postage stamp brought it all back.

Yes! I had found Arthur. We start shooting emails back and forth across the ocean, and he fills me in on some of the things I was dying to know about.

How does he tell how long a body has been sitting on the side of the road? Warm and floppy = just died. Cold and stiff = a few hours or a day. Belly going green and smelly = a few days. Of course it depends on the weather, too.

He tells me more about eating polecat. He used an old Italian recipe for fox that recommends you run the body under water for 4 days to get rid of the stink. Arthur says it makes polecat taste good.

Why does he eat roadkill? *One big advantage,* he writes, *is that it is organic, with not a trace of the hormones, antibiotics, and unnatural feedstuff given to so many farmed animals these days.* Another reason: he feels he's doing the right thing by removing bodies from the roadside. Plus, this lifestyle prevents animals from being butchered to provide him with sustenance.

"I'd do my utmost to avoid killing anything."

Man, I like this guy.[20] Isn't it interesting how a personal letter and a few email exchanges changed him in my mind from "Mr. Boyt" to "Arthur" and turned my skepticism into respect?

Arthur isn't the only one eating other people's roadkill. In Alaska, if you hit a moose, you are required by law to report it. The carcass becomes state property. The state troopers call it in to a charity organization. Then, some lucky volunteer rushes out to pick it up—not an easy task, seeing as the body can weigh 1,800 pounds. Then that guy delivers it to a butcher. There's no time to waste, because they've got to get it gutted, bled, and cooled before the bad germies get to work.[21] Lastly, the moose meat is donated to someone else who needs it.

When their teacher hauls in a roadkill moose, the students in the Moose Club at Su-Valley Junior High get in on the action. Cutting, skinning, processing, the students turn it into moose burgers and feed the hungry folks at the senior center across the street. Talk about sinking your teeth into your service project!

One school lunch program makes good use of roadkill moose meat, too. Ever wonder what's in that mystery meat?

After learning all this I'm still not planning on eating someone else's roadkill—meat that has been baking in the Alabama sun for who knows how long. But I have decided one thing. I've never hit a deer, thank goodness, but if I accidently do—and if it's legal to salvage the meat—I now intend to eat it.

---

[20] Arthur let me know he's writing his own book about roadkill. Can't wait to read that!
[21] But it is Alaska, so the cold weather helps some.

CHAPTER 9
Mama

I was driving around a curve on a little country road, one country store in sight, when I spotted a suitcase on the shoulder. Wait! Luggage? No. I whipped the car around and passed the suitcase on the other side. A turtle. A snapping turtle with one claw reaching out across the white line.

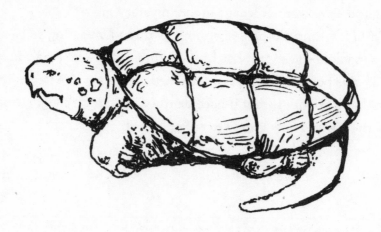

I turned around a second time and scanned for a safe place to stop. Why are roadkill always in the least safe place to rescue them?

Oh.

The *least* safe place. The place where cars have the least sight distance, the least stopping time, the least ability to avoid a foot-long turtle lumbering across the road.

O-o-o-o-h.

Then words swam up from the depths of my memory. David Laurencio saying something about turtles.

I had been standing there in the wet collections of the museum at Auburn, surrounded by all those jars. Something just behind me, at head height, had me turning and reaching for it. A large jar filled with round things strung together puzzled me. It looked as if 30 Ping-Pong balls had been jammed down into an old lady's pair of white hose and then twisted into knots.

The label read:

AUBURN UNIVERSITY MUSEUM

HERPETOLOGY COLLECTION

CHELYDRA SERPENTINA

AUM 40610[1]

ALABAMA

COLBERT COUNTY

"So," David had said, sighing, "that is roadkill. A female that got hit by a car. A snapping turtle." Aquatic turtles stay in their pond

---

[1] AUM is the code for this museum—every natural history museum's got one, and 40610 is the number assigned to this specimen.

or river most of the time. Females, David had told me, are the most likely to get hit because they leave the water to find a place for their nest.[2][3]

A mother. To think of the creatures those eggs could have become.

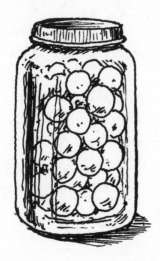

As I pulled my car off on the grass, the pieces started to click into place in my mind: early spring, turtle, nesting ...

I had to get that turtle off the road. That *mama* turtle. Her eyes swiveled toward me like a dinosaur in a movie. She was old-leather-suitcase brown and crusted in mud. Her neck looked like crinkled crepe paper, a squished-down turtleneck ... Duh, I guess that's where they got the name. A tail of a Stegosaurus—rigid plates jutted up like 2-D mountain ridges in two parallel lines running down her muscular appendage. Could she whack me with it?

Then I spotted her other side.

Cracks stairstepped across her shell like Earth's plates at a fault line. White fibers splintered out from the cracks, some frosted with red. A 3-inch tongue of pink throbbed from her shell. An organ? I

---

[2] One study found common snapping turtle nests an average of 39 meters from the water. One nest was 982 meters away from the water's edge. That's almost 9 football fields—a long way for little legs to travel—and there's a good chance mama turtle had to cross a road on that journey.

[3] Where that nest ends up matters. If a common snapping turtle's eggs are incubated at 68 degrees Fahrenheit, then females hatch out. At 70 to 72 degrees, males and females hatch; 73 to 75, all males. Those guys are hot stuff.

squatted to see. It was shiny, with a surface like plastic wrap, and lined with rootlike red veins. A bubble welled up from underneath. I winced to think of a bulge of my gut hanging out.

Her body was perched on the white line at the edge of the road. The line between life and death. Dark liquid ran downhill, picking its way toward the shoulder of the road.

A car whooshed toward us. Needing to move fast, I grabbed her tail.[4] I pulled up and dragged her onto the gravel. Her claws reached

out. Long. Longer than Piper's. Shouts and chaos spilled from the windows of a school bus that slowed to a stop at the country store.

Crouching on the shoulder, we were still in the belly of that

---

[4] Never, *ever* pick up a turtle by its tail! I cringe remembering the *pop-pop-pop* sounds I heard—probably her vertebrae dislocating. Now I know better, and use a car mat to drag big turtles across the road.

curve. The least safe place. No good. Behind me was a little pond, probably her pond. I hefted her once more and plopped her—trying to do it gently, but she was heavy—onto the grassy bank. The smell of spring. The sound of someone mowing early spring grass. The damp air of the pond.

As I stared at her splintered shell, my eyelids began to burn. All those eggs.[5]

David had explained how scientists use eggs from roadkill. "These give us 2 bits of information: a clutch[6] size for that turtle, and a time. The more clutches you have with dates on them, the more data you can compile, and you have a better feel for what you know." If, in September, you found 1 turtle that was about to lay eggs, you might assume that species reproduces in September. But if instead you found 10 turtles, you might discover that they actually reproduce from June to October. You might need a sample size of 50 turtles to be confident you're on the right track.

You could learn a lot from a clutch of eggs, but as I ran my fingers along that mama's splintered spine, data didn't matter. The turtle gaped up at me. I *had* to do something. I'd take her to a wildlife rehabilitation center, a place that can fix broken animals. I whipped out the phone and typed in "Alabama reptile rehab" and found a nice list entitled "Current Wildlife Rehabbers." Grasshoppers twirred nearby as I scrolled down the chart, reading the descriptions of the different types of injured animals each place would accept:

---

[5] As the number of roads increase over time, the ratio of female-to-male aquatic turtles is changing. Fewer females. Fewer females = fewer baby turtles.

[6] *Clutch*: all the eggs laid together in one nest.

- mammals, small mammals, deer, squirrels
- deer, opossum, and other non-RVS species[7]
- deer and other mammals
- hawks, owls, eagles, vultures, and other raptor species

What? Did no one care about reptiles?! Of the 58 listings, just 1 was a possibility: "All native animals, including deer (including rabies vector species)." I punched in their number. All I got was a recording. Checking the time, I realized it was after hours.

I thought, fleetingly, of carrying her with me to the conference I was headed to. But no. I couldn't. I didn't know how to care for her. She and all her eggs needed medical care; even a regular vet wouldn't know what to do with her.[8]

Should I move her closer to the water? Would that make her feel better, more at home? The thought of picking her up again, of grinding that fractured fault line together again, grated at my nerves. I couldn't. Besides, that water was surely full of bacteria.

Looking at her mud-caked shell, I should have realized it wouldn't make things any worse.

The sun was starting to dip. My mental clock was ticking.

Suddenly, I was angry at those cars slipping by in their

---

[7] *Non-RVS species* = non-rabies vector species. A vector is an organism that carries a disease, so those organizations only accept animals that can't carry rabies—the nasty virus that's spread through spit and causes your brain to swell and makes you fear water.
[8] Thanks to a law that lets vets perform emergency care, one "regular" vet I learned about was able to rescue an injured box turtle. When someone brought her the turtle with a triangle of shell floating around unattached to the rest of the shell, Dr. Shannon Moore did some quick thinking. She sent someone to the auto store. Dr. Moore sealed the shell up with a fiberglass patch kit. Because the turtle didn't have other internal injuries, she thought it had a chance, and released it. Several years later, walking in that turtle's territory, she was amazed to find that very patient plodding along living a happy life, fiberglass and all.

aerodynamic bliss, walled off from the world—her world—of pain. This one turtle did nothing to deserve this. This one little turtle. This one *mama turtle*, just trying to find a sandy spot to nestle her precious little ones.

No one else knows about her. No one thinks, *Oh, I'm coming to a potentially dangerous area, an area where the road veers near water.* No one thinks, *This is a sensitive time—early spring, when many animals are taking the risk of a lifetime and venturing out of their safe, comfort zones (off their couches and into a scary world), at 5 p.m., when the human traffic, too, is busier—*

I am one of those drivers. My body jolted as my rear end hit the ground. *I am one* of those drivers.

Infographics scrolled through my head:

- 870 million vehicles on the planet
- 64 million kilometers of road[9]
- 2 million animals hit
- 200 humans dead

The numbers felt like a stack of pizza boxes reaching to the sky.

And all those uses of roadkill—the parts for art, the flesh for food, the scientific specimens? They didn't stack up. They just couldn't compensate.

That stack of facts was leaning, leaning, and any moment would come crashing down on me.

I slid that mama turtle to the edge of her pond and dragged myself back to my car. In anger, I cranked the engine and headed up the road. Tears carved canyons down my cheeks.

---

[9] Enough for 83 trips to the moon and back!

Maybe I'm too much of an optimist, but over the next few weeks, something kept trying to pull the splinters of my hope back together. My heart and my mind were reaching out for a solution. The more I thought about roadkill, the longer that weight sat on my heart, the more it sunk in that it wasn't about one mama turtle or even all her eggs. It wasn't about saving one endangered species. This problem of roadkill—it's an epidemic. And I couldn't fathom that humans were ignoring that kind of tragedy.

The words of Dr. Shilling came back to me: the single largest human cause of death among wild animals is vehicles.

But wait. There are entire campaigns to stop people from using plastic drinking straws.[10] Laws have been proposed to make it a criminal act to release helium balloons.[11] People dedicate their entire lives to helping us understand the lives and family dynamics of chimpanzees.[12] Humans care. They go to great lengths—and depths—to save animals.[13]

But roadkill? Where's the concern about that? What was I

---

[10] And one of those was created and run by 2 amazing teenagers who knew that plastic straws can end up in the wrong place, like in the nostril of an endangered sea turtle.

[11] Protect those birds and sea turtles!

[12] Can you say, "Thank you, Jane Goodall!"?

[13] There's one guy who cares so much about turtles, he gave one mouth-to-mouth resuscitation *and it worked!*

missing? There had to be *someone* out there doing *something* about it.[14]

And that's when I thought of Big Dave.

At the McDowell Environmental Center, where I used to work, one of their classes included information about wildlife-vehicle collisions. For some reason, elbow deep in all this roadkill research, I had forgotten about it. I could have relied on my memories of that class, but my memory was kind of foggy, and their senior naturalist, Big Dave, is kind of magical, so I went back to McDowell to watch him in action.

I sat in a large room with 100 sweaty fifth graders, waiting for the show to begin.

"Ugh, ugh, ugh—*Ugh!*" David Holloway threw out both hands in sideways peace symbols, and the kids went nuts. "*Awesome!*" A trio of girls in the front row did the "Big Dave hands" and giggled.

I don't know why, Dave doesn't know why, the kids don't know why, but his grunt-stance-hand-signal combo is like a magnet to any crowd. Dave, Joel (pronounced *ho-EL*), and their feathered friends were doing a presentation called Radical Raptors.[15] The birds had been injured and rehabilitated but had never recovered enough to return to the wild.

Dave was warming up the crowd and giving them some warnings about how to act when he or Joel brings out a live animal. "Young people, they will scat right in front of you." *Scat* is just another word for "poo." "If that happens, please don't fall on the floor. Please don't *stare* at it." It was like he didn't want the birds to be embarrassed.

---

[14] At that point in my quest, I hadn't yet met Fraser and all his road-ecology buddies.
[15] Dinosaurs? No, the modern kind—birds like hawks, owls, and eagles.

For 10 minutes, Joel and Dave awed the crowd with phenomenal facts about those dinosaur descendants. Then the duo carried out a red-tailed hawk, an American kestrel, and a great horned owl, and blew our minds some more.

When one bird squirted on the floor, Joel asked, "Did she go number one or number two?" Kids stifled giggles and gave all kinds of answers. "Trick question—she did number three. Both at the same time."

A great horned owl's grip can be over 400 pounds per square inch. As Big Dave puts it, that's stronger than the grips of 4 humans put together.

Big Dave had the owl perched on his wrist. "Her favorite food? This dude who lives in the woods." Dave made a show of holding his nose.

"Skunks!" the kids whisper-shouted.[16]

"This is a skunk-eating machine! Awesome! Skunk is like pepperoni pizza to her. That cool musk gland a skunk has? Doesn't work on her. A great horned owl has no sense of smell."

Then Dave's face got serious. His hand stroked his beard. His voice dropped to almost a whisper. "The American kestrel got hit by a car, lost an eye, and lost a wing. The red-tailed hawk had head injuries and wing injuries that did not heal properly. They are non-releasable. The great horned owl, she, too, got hit by a car. She had a broken wing, she had severe head injuries, and she broke a toe. And she lost one of her eyes."

The crowd was absolutely still. A watch beeped. People glared at the owner.

---

[16] Can you imagine how loud a real shout would be to an owl?

"Guys, she had to dedicate her life to being a teacher. Her message? 'Please don't feed the highway.'" The boys beside me looked at each other with puzzled expressions.

"Throwing food out the car window is devastating our wildlife. Tons of people are like 'Dude! I would never litter. I would never toss a piece of paper out my window.' But an apple core?" He mimicked tossing a core into the crowd. "French fries?" *Flick, flick.* "Our raptors would never eat an apple core. But, guys, in nature, all things are connected. A possum, a mouse, a rat, a skunk—would they eat apple cores or french fries? Absolutely."

Dave looked at the owl, who serenely surveyed the audience. "If she learns to go every single day to the highway as a hunting post, is she going to make it to 15 years old?" The owl slowly blinked.[17]

"Grown-ups"—Big Dave turned to the row of chaperones—"did you know that throwing food out the window was bad? I didn't." He shook his head. "But *knowledge* is *power.*"

I sat there, watching one hundred pairs of human eyes riveted by the owl. One hundred pairs of ears hanging on every word. One hundred hearts reaching out to that bird. Big Dave was *doing* something about roadkill. He was doing something *powerful.* Big Dave had transformed a tragic situation into a story that could help prevent it from happening again.

---

[17] Owls have a third eyelid called a nictitating membrane. It is a clear protective covering and closes diagonally from the inside to the outside of the eye.

CHAPTER 10

Dodging Death

High on a hill in the middle of Oak Mountain State Park, the Alabama Wildlife Center occupied an abandoned restaurant. It is a conservation organization that reused, recycled, and renewed. How fitting.

The building seemed to take a higher view of things, looking down on the everyday world where every day animals get crunched. The parking lot was a quiet void in the early spring forest of naked limbs and paintbrush-tipped pines. Someone carted a load of trash to a dumpster. Little did I realize then that several hours later that lonely piece of pavement would etch itself into my brain forever.

This is where birds[1] who have been hit go when they just might make it! Animals that might be able to skip death—at least for a little while. This is the kind of place Big Dave's birds came from. Would I see someone actually *fix* an animal? Bring one back to life?! I should

---

[1] The center is actually all about birds—songbirds and raptors, for the most part.

have been charging in the door to see all that action, but instead, the forest called to me. The leaf-lush forest floor sucked at my toes. The inhale of earth, damp and full of pine pollen, lured me toward it.

Or maybe it was just that I knew heart-stabs might be hiding behind those dark doors. According to the center's website, almost 2,000 injured or orphaned birds are brought in each year.

All hope to fly out.

Two-thirds of them don't.

Dodging death isn't guaranteed.

But the clock was ticking, and soon I could put it off no longer. I headed toward the building. Along the sidewalk, black letters shouted out from a crisp white sign:

QUIET! HOSPITAL ZONE
Patients need quiet to heal.

In the entryway, a man in a fleece vest, button-down shirt, and khakis strode toward me and extended his hand. Doug Adair reminded me of a great horned owl. Wise and in charge, he spoke as if he were leading a school tour.

Two young professionals, Scottie Jackson and Katie Stubblefield, joined us. Scottie, the educator of the group, had hair as bouncy as her personality. She's a barred owl,[2] for sure. Perky, smiling broadly, and gushing with passion for her work. Hooded under a ball cap, Katie was as focused as a red-tailed hawk. As Doug talked, Katie swayed back and forth, impatient with our chitter-chatter, her hands fidgeting with neon key rings. No earrings, no frills—she's a

---

[2] Barred owls seem friendly and social. They send their spooky question out into the air, day or night, always up for a chat: *"Who-cooks-for-you-whooo-cooks-for-you-alllll?"*

"Let's get down to business" kind of gal. I get that! Her T-shirt was flecked with white bits of something. Food from a bird feeding? Bedding? Flakes of raptor flesh?

"We might have a patient in that category," Doug was saying, "and we'd be thrilled if—" A volunteer burst through the swinging doors behind Doug and leaned in to ask him a question.

Wait! My mind scrambled. What category? Thrilled if *what*? Scribbling notes, I had missed what Doug was talking about.

Minutes later, we were in the converted kitchen. Right where a cook once prepared a steak dinner, a volunteer now sliced and diced mouse parts. Intensive-care birds get only the juiciest parts.

Scottie told me a bit more about her role: "We educate because we hope it will eventually reduce our intake.[3] Every animal that comes to this facility is connected to a human being. Whoever found it. Whoever's little girl wrapped it in a blanket and put it in a shoe box. They get to go home and tell a friend, 'I saved an animal's life today.'"

"Seeing all these injured animals, what does it make you think about when you're driving?" I asked.

"It makes you pay attention," Scottie said. "If we see roadkill on the road, we scoot it off the road and into the woods. It's such a danger to other animals.

"We see more vultures come in with car-strike injuries than any other injury. Roadkill is a real hazard to those guys. It's a nice, easy meal right in the middle of a big, open space. They just want to stick their heads right down in it and chow down.[4] Then they become victims."

---

[3] They use the language of a hospital: *intake, patients, recovery,* for example.
[4] Their bald heads allow all that sticky stuff to slide right off after their meal.

Once we were in the exam room, Katie came out of her shell. "One hundred percent of our screech owls are car impacts. Over 70 percent of large waterfowl and raptors are car impacts. Most of them you can just tell by the injuries—head trauma, eye injuries—a couple were pulled directly from the grille of a car." A picture from my internet research flashed through my brain: a bald eagle's head and wing sticking out from the bumper of an SUV. Amazingly, that bird made it. How? Who knows.

The room was small and crammed with stuff: boxes of medical supplies, crates of forms, a metal scale, a strange pile of equipment with hoses sticking out every which way. Permits hung in tidy black frames on the wall. A cabinet full of tiny drawers reminded me of the one in my grandpa's workshop, except his was full of screws. Imagine what might be behind those little white labels: needles, blades, all kinds of sharp, pointy stuff. The spray bottles marked CLEANING made me wonder how much blood this room had seen. The exam table was not much different from the one at Piper's vet's office.

Then I noticed a scratching sound at my feet. We looked down. The sound coming from a cardboard box[5] told us that somebody was getting impatient . . .

Scottie pulled on thick brown leather

---

[5] A $1.50 cardboard box—not really a "high-tech" enclosure, but the box can be reused if not too much gets smeared on it . . .

gloves that reached almost to her elbows. She pulled a 2-foot form out of the box. A blue dish towel covered the bird's head to keep the bird calm. Katie wrestled around a minute and soon had a fluffy brown owl tucked against her belly. His talons were held firmly in her hands. Not only were they razor-sharp, they could close with enough pressure to crush a skull. Brains for breakfast, anyone?

Katie pulled off the towel.

Cool yellow eyes stared forward. A hooked black beak jutted out, its edges as sharp as glass. The owl was brown, but not completely. Individual feathers were yellow, white, black, and gray. Feathers so fine they looked like hairs radiated from his eyes in a sunburst pattern. Darker plumes stood straight up as 2 tufts on his forehead.

A great horned owl! Magnificent, wild, with an air of royalty about him.

Katie went to work checking his legs, wings, feathers, eyes, mouth, ears, and basic functions. She felt his keel, the breastbone that stuck forward from within his chest. She said you could get a quick assessment of his health by checking that. His flight muscles were nice and plump beside the keel. If he'd been without food or water, they would have been caved in.

This owl was found on the ground near a church, but great horneds don't hang out on the ground. There were no solid clues as to what had happened to him, but when Katie found crunchiness[6] in his shoulder, we all suspected a car strike.

"We will have to send it for an X-ray because it could be a fracture. And that could be really bad, because fractures in the joint don't really heal. And that will mean he would lose his mobility..."

---

[6] Just the sound of that makes me cringe.

His "ears"[7] laid back like Piper's do when she's unhappy about getting her nails clipped. Katie wrapped his wing in a splint that looked like a figure eight.

Without any fancy equipment, she had checked, diagnosed, and stabilized this patient in less than 10 minutes. It was a good thing, too, because in came a volunteer toting a large plastic box sealed shut with electrical tape:[8] "I'm bringing you a new bird, a red-tailed hawk."

"What happened to him?"

The volunteer sighed. "Best bet, he got hit by a car."

Red-tails, Katie explained as she tucked the owl back into a crate, are notorious for getting hit twice.

Twice?

They get hit by a car. Injured and unable to fly, they survive by eating roadkill. This puts them in the perfect position to get hit again. Double whammy.

"They are one of the few birds we get in that are emaciated,"[9] she went on, "because they can go for so long just scavenging on the side of the road."

"There's something to be said about convenience," Scottie jumped in, "even for the healthy ones. Think about it: Would you rather go to the fast-food drive-through or have to chase your hamburger through the woods?"

---

[7] The tufts on his head are not ears—they're just feathers that make him look like a broken-off tree. His true ears are flat against the sides of his head, hidden under feathers that funnel sound to them.

[8] Birds come in all kinds of containers. One big, burly man needed to keep a baby bluebird warm on the trip to the center, so he strapped on his wife's bra and tucked the little guy inside. His body heat probably saved the bird's life. That's my kind of macho man.

[9] *Emaciated:* extremely thin from lack of food or water.

Oh, that makes sense.

Scottie brought in another red-tailed hawk, one that had been at the center for a few days. Soon she had me sticking my fingers into the soft warm feathers on its breast. She wanted me to assess the bird's general health based on its keel.

"Oh my gosh, it feels like a knife edge." No nice plump flight muscles on that guy. Katie pointed to an X-ray. Between his knee and his ankle, one of the bones was broken into 4 separate pieces.

Yikes.

"I'm hoping we can align it and it can callous[10] back in. I'm not sure the vet can pin it."

She planned to send the hawk to the doctor the next week, but the surgeons were backed up. You see, vets donate their time to work on the raptors. Paying customers get to go first.

"When he came in," Katie said, "his foot was flopping off to the side. It was difficult to splint."

"What happens if you can't?" I asked.

"Then we have to do a humane euthanasia."[11]

We all fell silent as Katie fashioned a new splint. She sandwiched the leg between 2 flat pieces of wood—they looked like craft sticks—and bound them in place with a bright yellow wrap.

---

[10] She means that the edges of the bones knit back together.
[11] The formal way to say ending its life to put it out of its misery.

I squirmed at the thought of asking the next question, but I had to know: "If you have to do that"—I squirmed again at the thought of this sleek beauty, this feisty fighter, this eager life being extinguished—"what do you do with the body?"

"We have a couple of options." I could tell Scottie had answered this question before. "One is that we have proper disposal techniques,[12] but in some cases we can donate the body—transfer it to permitted educators to use. The animal can still have a purpose even if things don't work out the way we want them to."

After the patient assessments, Katie gave me a tour through the rest of the facility. There was a mallard duck that had been struck by a car near Hoover Library. An albino[13] vulture who had been kicked out of her flock. And bird after bird after bird who didn't win when they went head-to-head with a car. Hey, why put all the blame on the cars? Trucks, planes, trains[14]—they all do it too.

Katie said that vehicle collisions aren't the only problems roads cause. Loons, coots, and other waterbirds can get trapped on asphalt roads. Imagine a migrating bird who has just flapped hundreds of miles, coming in for a rest on what looks like a nice, smooth stretch of river. Only, when they go to splash down, the river turns out to be asphalt. The landing is probably a shock, but the real issue crops up when they try to leave.

"They usually use their legs to practically run across the water for up to 300 yards before they can take flight. But on the road, they can't. So they get stuck on the asphalt river."

---

[12] She means that they incinerate the body, burning any germs it might have carried.

[13] Albino animals don't have any pigment; they are perfectly white. I guess her "buddies" weren't cool with someone who dressed differently.

[14] Elk like train tracks because there's less snow to plow through. Unfortunately, when a train going 60 miles per hour hits an elk, the animal kind of explodes.

In one bird pen, dead white mice were scattered on wooden stairs that had been covered in plastic grass. Floppy pink tails dangled in thin air. It looked kind of ghoulish, but I knew the birds needed to eat. Earlier, I had seen the freezer crammed with frozen mice. The nine injured owls in there—seven of them were car impacts with eye injuries[15] or brain trauma[16]—could hop on up to their frozen dinner.

Once we had seen every nook and cranny of the center, Katie and Scottie armed themselves with a net like the long-handled ones at a swimming pool. They headed for the red-tailed hawk flight enclosure. They'd been hinting all afternoon about a bird that might be ready for release, but first they had to catch her. If the hawk is all healed up—well enough to swerve, dart, and swoop to catch wild animals—catching her should not be easy.

✗ ✗ ✗

"You got your gloves?" Scottie asked. It had taken about 20 minutes of chasing and flushing and patience, but Katie and Scottie had finally nabbed the red-tailed hawk. Now we were back in the exam room, where they were preparing her for release.

"I've got my gloves." I looked down at the faded red leather, creased and stained with greasy bits. "I'm official."

But why did I need gloves?

Katie started telling me this bird's history. "It was a long, arduous treatment. You are talking about surgery, time, and money, especially donations on the vet's part. So, we are really fortunate to

---

[15] If an owl loses sight in 1 eye, and everything else is okay, the center will release it back into the wild. An owl's hearing is so good that it can hunt in the dark with just 1 eye.

[16] In cartoons, when a critter gets run over, they always show it as if the brain is spinning. In real life, it is more like sloshing. The soft gray matter of the brain smashes against the inside of that hard skull. Ouch.

get her ready to go. Four months is a long time. It's a huge, huge commitment."

She came to the center in early November, with bones so mangled that a normal treatment wouldn't do. The vet had to install an apparatus on the outside of the bird's body that looked like an erector set with rods, clamps, and bolts holding it all together. It required 3 different pins inside the wing, and 2 surgeries. The wing took 2 months to heal; then she needed another 2 months in the cage to practice flying again. When they had thought she was finally ready, she molted her feathers. So they had to wait even longer till she was good to go.

Once the bird was checked and prepped, we made our way outside, gathering volunteers and cameras along the way.

These people were *doing something* about roadkill. They had changed this bird's story for life.

"This is exciting!" I said as Scottie guided me through the parking lot.

"From being wild, doing her thing, to being hit and in all that pain, now she's about to taste freedom for the first time in months. It's a huge thing when you are only a year or 2 old."

"Katie, what about over there, out of the shadow?" Doug directed us to go farther away from the dumpster and the telephone lines. We were all eager for him to get a slow-motion video of the moment with his phone.

"I'm not releasing her," Katie retorted.

My heart jumped.

"I'm handing her off."

Before I could think, Katie started giving me instructions—today, writing this, my heart starts pounding just remembering that moment—where to put my hand, how to hold the bird, how to let her go. I practiced, thinking of my fingers gripping those strong, talon-tipped yellow legs. What if I squeezed her too tight? What if I dropped her?

"Don't toss her," Katie said. "Just open both hands. Like this." Except she didn't let the hawk go.

Then Katie handed me the bird—just like that. Her head was draped in a green towel to keep her calm. But what about me? It was happening so fast. I fumbled in the too-thick gloves, but eventually I got my right hand around the scaly legs. I kept her beak pointed away from my body and pressed the backs of her wings against my chest.

Katie slid the towel off.

I'm really doing it, I thought, *holding this wild animal. Squinting into the evening sun, just like she is.* Those paintbrush-tipped pines were calling to her.

Her wings hunched up like a kid squirming to get out of a hug that goes on too long. Her head swiveled left then right. *What is she thinking?*

I counted down. "Three." *Oh my gosh, I can't believe I'm holding this bird.*

Ring.

Heads swiveled to see whose phone it was.

"Two."

Ring. .

"Oh no." Doug stared at his phone. "Wait. Hang on, let me just— Okay, I'm back." He repositioned his phone, ready to take the video. At least 3 other cameras were held ready in midair.

"One!" I shoved the bird into the space in front of me.

Flap, flap, flap.

The group erupted.

"Awesome!"

"Live!"

"Wow!"

Volunteers, staff, and I stood, agape at the way her wings lifted her up, up, up. She crossed the pavement and perched in a pine. Looking back, I can't help wondering if she feared the sight and smell of pavement.

My heart lifted with her. I imagined the wind ruffling her feathers, pine scent and pollen filling her nares.[17] That parking lot didn't feel so lonely anymore. It felt as if I were in a movie. I was playing a part—a small part, but a part nonetheless—in this miracle of recovery.

Today, *telling* you about it doesn't feel like enough. Like it was so profound that my words won't do it justice. But that day, as smiles passed from face to face, they showed it all.

Thirty minutes later, I settled into my sunbaked car, thinking, *Tonight that glorious animal who was smashed by a car and* almost died *will be back where she belongs.*

I pulled out my phone and posted: *Best research day ever!*

---

[17] *Nares*: the bird word for "nostrils."

CHAPTER 11

Trees, Tolls, and Tweets

Imagine you are a panther pacing along a dry, gritty ledge. A rugged mountain towers dark and inviting in the night behind you, but you can't go back. That belongs to another lion. An older, wiser, larger lion. You can't go forward, either. A wall of wheels confronts you. Sixteen lanes worth of spinning, screeching, and honking. What's a cat to do?

My visit to the Alabama Wildlife Center had given me hope, but let's get real—most animals who are hit aren't so lucky: 1) they are killed on impact; or 2) there might not be a rehab center open to them; or 3) volunteers and rehabbers work with them for months but the animal still dies. That kind of after-the-fact solution wasn't good enough. In comparison to all the death, it was just a little bitty bandage slapped on a big festering sore. I needed more than that.

That's why I found myself standing on a mountain slope in Southern California thinking about entire populations of mountain lions[1] who are fenced in by pavement. There's one cat, P22,[2] who's got himself stuck in a city park. You'd think that having the entire 6.5-square-mile Griffith Park to himself—and all those yummy deer—would be a good thing. He's hanging out under the Hollywood Sign—who could ask for more than that? But a male panther needs 75 to 200 square miles to stretch his legs. And then there are all those roads roaring right around him.[3] Besides that, this guy needs a mate.

Oddly, instead of being filled with dread at the thought of this kitty smacked by a car, hope was beginning to bubble up within me. Hope generated by people like Mark Lotz, Doug Feremenga, and Beth Pratt-Bergstrom, who are all doing phenomenal things to put the brakes on panther-vehicle collisions.

Take Mark Lotz, for example. He's up at 4 a.m., tromping around in the swamps of the Everglades (mosquitoes, poison ivy, pythons,

---

[1] Although they are called "mountain lions," these cats aren't lions at all. They can't roar, they don't live in prides, and they don't have bushy manes. Technically, they are more closely related to my kitty cat.

[2] Puma 22: He was the 22nd mountain lion captured by the biologists of the Santa Monica Mountains National Park Service.

[3] Griffith Park is sandwiched between the 5, the 134, and the 101 freeways. Scientists figure that to get to the park, P22 had to have braved some of the nation's nastiest traffic nightmares, like the 405 freeway—a traffic artery that always flows even at prime mountain lion time—the middle of the night. How did he do it? We'll never know. Maybe his 40-foot leap helped.

and all) with trained dogs and a crew all working hard to track down Florida panthers.[4] Once the dogs chase a cat up a tree, someone shoots it.

No, not with bullets! Tranquilizer darts.

The crew moves quickly to slide a crash bag and a cargo net directly under the cat. What if kitty settles into a crotch in the tree and falls asleep, instead of into the waiting net?

Mark straps on spikes and climbs up, up, up the flagpole pine. High enough that the people below look like munchkins. Once he safely lowers the sleeping panther into the net, the crew takes measurements, plucks hairs, draws blood, and injects vaccinations. Then they strap on a GPS collar. What's that got to do with roadkill?

Depressing Panther Headlines of 2017:

---

[4] Panthers, pumas, cougars, mountain lions? Which name is right? It depends on where you are. All these big cats are the same species, *Puma concolor*. Florida panthers are a subspecies of that species. Remember those southern and northern coyotes, and how they are a bit different from each other? Cats can do it too. Once upon a time these big cats ran free across almost all of North and South America. But as humans moved in, cats moved out. Just like my kitty does when company comes.

- January 13: "First Panther Death, Roadkill of 2017 Reported," *News-Press*
- March 15: "Sixth Panther Road Kill of the Year Recorded," *Daily Tribune, Wisconsin Rapids*
- April 10: "Panther Roadkill in Hendry Marks 10th Big Cat of the Year," *USA Today*
- May 11: "Panther Road Kill Marks 13th Recorded Big Cat Death of the Year," *Argus Leader*
- June 19: "Panther Roadkill in Hendry Marks 15th Big Cat Death of the Year," *Florida Today*[5]

This news is like an ad that loops over and over. It's so repetitious, it's not "new" news, and writers just copy the old headlines. The numbers just click on by like white dashes on the highway. At one point, the Florida panther population was down to 20–30 animals, so low that they had to import cats from Texas to keep the population healthy.

But Mark's on the job. He is the Florida panther biologist for the Florida Fish and Wildlife Conservation Commission. Since 1981, the commission has been working to save this endangered species. Using GPS locations emailed from the collars and the very high frequency (VHF) functionality, Mark spies on the kitties from a plane. He wants to know if they are taking advantage of secret

---

[5] There are plenty more headlines, but I don't have the heart to include them all.

tunnels—tunnels people have built for big cat paws![6] Way back in 1972, when people were planning to build a new interstate that would slice through prime panther territory near the Everglades, it was obvious that the cats and the cars would not play well together. So, as the government built that road, they installed 24 wildlife crossings. Some looked like big culverts; some turned the road into a bridge over dry land. All were ways for animals to sneak safely under the road.

The Florida panther population has grown to about 120–130. How cool is that?

✗ ✗ ✗

I checked into it, and Florida's not the only place digging safe spaces for wildlife. It turns out, people all over the world are doing it:

- France coughed up €65,000 ($77,000) to install tunnels where 1,200 frogs and toads used to get splattered each year.
- In New Zealand, little blue penguins now waddle safely through concrete culverts on their way home from a hard day of fishing.[7]
- And that spot in Canada where 75,000 garter snakes[8] gather to spend their winter in

---

[6] Of course, other animals scoot through the tunnels too. A mama bear with her cubs, possums, a red fox—just think if *my* red fox had had one of those!

[7] Where little blues don't have to cross a road, their commute takes 5 minutes. For this colony that faced busy Waterfront Road, the commute was 40 minutes—we all know about traffic—and lots of risk.

[8] Fun fact: with a single flick of his tongue, a guy garter can tell if another snake is a female, if she is from his den, and if she's likely to produce lots of babies or just a few.

sinkholes? Some years 25,000 of them became snake-ment. In 1994, the government got busy fixing that. Their bright idea—snow fences to guide the snakes into existing drainage culverts for safe crossing.[9] By 2000, with a few more culverts, they had cut the snake deaths by 75 percent.[10]

There's just one little problem with tunnels. Animals don't always love them.[11] They can be dark and wet and weird and loud.[12]

"Sometimes," said Doug Feremenga, "you have an underpass right there, and an animal gets hit 50 feet from it." Dr. Doug Feremenga is an urban environmental planner for the Transportation Corridor Agencies (TCA) in California, but originally he's from Zimbabwe. Back in the 1990s TCA built the 241 toll road through the Santa Ana Mountains where a population of mountain lions lived.

I had heard plenty of people rave about Doug's award-winning fence. A fence? I hopped a plane and flew across the continent to see why people were making such a big deal about a fence.

Don't let Doug's fancy title, button-up oxford, or neatly braided hair give you the wrong impression; he swapped his city-slicker

---

[9] They even heated one culvert to see if that lured in more snakes.
[10] Not perfect, but I bet there was a lot of happy hissing going on.
[11] Once, I tried to get Piper to go through a culvert with me. She would have nothing to do with it. Instead, she climbed straight up the steep bank and sat in the middle of the road. Her look said, "This way is simpler, silly." She hates getting her paws wet.
[12] One scientist has questions about some perfectly good underpasses that mountain lions refuse to use. He's testing out the decibel levels with sound-frequency equipment. Maybe kitty-cat ears are sensitive to sounds we humans don't even hear.

shoes for hiking boots, and he took me right out into the mountains. We stood in Oak Canyon, the harsh sun beating on my shoulders, the dry wind turning my skin to lizard scales. Oak Canyon is one of the most important corridors for lions in Southern California. You see, the freeways around the rest of the Santa Anas wall those big cats off from the world. A prison for pumas.

Remember that piece about the Samango monkeys and what happens when young guys can't go their own way?

Santa Ana Population: 20 (mountain lions)

"We were starting to see physical manifestations of the genetic confinement," Doug said. "They are confined by the roads, so really closely related animals are beginning to mate. You have sister plus brother, cousin plus cousin, so then the gene pool starts to get really, really undiluted."

Now, I called it Doug's fence, but actually it is now owned by the people of California, and you have to understand that building this thing was not a one-man deal. It took biologists and engineers and planners and geographers and marketers and construction workers and... To learn about the fence, I only spoke to Doug and Dr. Winston Vickers, but an entire team of folks from many different organizations worked together to make it happen. And they designed it based on ideas other projects had tested out.

According to Winston Vickers, this population of lions might have the least genetic diversity of any in California. And he should know. This vet-turned-mountain-lion-expert and his collaborators have been studying them, their DNA, and their characteristics for over 15 years.[13] "When we start seeing physical abnormalities such

---

[13] I'm betting some of what Winston knows came from museum specimens like David's.

as kinked tails,[14] cleft palates,[15] and weird hair patterns," Winston tells me, "those are like danger signals. We don't know for sure, but it is pretty strong evidence of physical changes associated with inbreeding."

Only 3 individuals have moved into this population since Winston started studying them. Only 1 of those successfully mated before he became DOR. I'm thinking how sad it was for that individual cat. Winston is pointing out how bad it was for the population. "Even 1 excess animal dying can whittle down such a small population. Each individual starts to become pretty important."

That's why it was a really good thing that the 241 toll road jumped right across Oak Canyon on a bridge so that cars wouldn't have to wind their way down in and back up out of the canyon. A bridge that left plenty of room for pumas to slink safely down the bottom of the canyon, under the wheels—but not *under* the wheels.

But that's not exactly how it happened.

The entire 51-mile toll road network was designed with wildlife underpasses at regular intervals, but still, ten cats have been killed. Ten cats extinguished forever. Ten sets of DNA removed from the gene pool. And there were great big underpasses right there!

That was not okay, so a team got busy building a wildlife exclusion fence. A fence to guide the animals to the underpasses. Just

---

[14] The pictures of kinked tails will give you a queasy feeling. Tails aren't supposed to take 90-degree turns.

[15] People can have cleft palates too. When the face doesn't join together properly during development, you get an opening from the roof of the mouth into the nose. People can have surgery to fix it. Wild cats can't.

any old playground fence wouldn't do. This had to be a special fence.[16]

"Mountain lions can have a vertical leap of up to 15 feet," Doug said. "And a horizontal leap of up to 20 feet.[17]" Looking up at the steep hillside, I imagine a lion leaping right over my head. I walk to the edge of the road and look straight up the fence. In some spots, it's 12 feet,[18] higher than a basketball hoop.

"And if they have an incentive, if a deer is on the other side, mountain lions can leap over fences pretty easily . . . and they are good climbers— maybe even better climbers than they are jumpers—which is why we had to put up these outriggers with strands of barbed wire."

Three prickly strands of barbed wire run along the top, angled toward the

---

[16] This fence shows off how much people have learned about animal behavior. At the end of the fence, you'd think it would just stop and deer would go around it. But thanks to Winston's knowledge of natural history, he told Doug the end of the fence should curve. Doug was like, "What?" but they tried it. Now the tip end bends away from the road. Deer trotting along the fence follow the curve and just keep curving away from the road even when there is no more fence.

[17] Doug said 20 feet—other people say 40 or 45 feet is a more accurate number for how far a mountain lion can jump. Even experts can disagree!

[18] The fence has to be taller in some spots to compensate for a hillside that could give the animals a good jumping-off spot.

wild lands. Now, I love the challenge of a tough climb, but I can't fathom getting safely over that, even if I were going the easy direction. Earlier, Doug had shown me how they chose a fence with diagonal spaces instead of flat squares, one more way to make it tougher for kitty-cat claws. They think of everything![19]

But jumpers and climbers weren't the only concern. Coyotes dig. The team buried the bottom of the fence 2 feet deep. They weren't cutting any corners.

This is probably the most carefully designed fence I'd ever laid my eyes (or hands) on,[20] and the most expensive, too—$10 million for both sides of this 6-mile stretch.

How many tolls does that take? That's a lot of money. Money that could be used for all kinds of important things. Is a fence worth it? And by now you know how my questions go—each one brings up more questions. This one brought up a really big one: How far do we go to prevent roadkill?

"In the first year of post-construction monitoring, we had 100 percent reduction for mountain lion roadkill, 100 percent for deer, 100 percent for bobcats, and 93 percent for coyotes," Doug explained.

Of all the studies I had read and heard of, not one could quote statistics that impressive. This fence was not only saving individual mountain lions; it was saving an entire population. But still, part of

---

[19] And I mean *everything*. What if an animal accidentally gets in? The team designed jump-out ramps—gaps in the fence where an animal can jump down safely from the road—but built high enough that from the wild side, a cat can't jump in. What about climbing in? They've got that covered. The top rung of wood that supports the ramp can be loosened so it's like a monkey bar that won't stop spinning when you try to grip it. So smart!

[20] They even thought to distress the metal so that it wasn't bright and shiny, and would blend into the surroundings.

me wondered: $10 million for *a fence*? Even me, animal-loving me, can't help but question that price tag.

When I ask him about it, Doug put it in terms of dollars and cents: "They say on average in the US it costs about $8,000, and that was in 2011 dollars." It takes me a minute to realize "it" meant the costs to repair a vehicle after it collides with a large mammal. I guess that makes cents *and* sense. You start multiplying that number by the number of roadkill, and insurance companies will tell you how quickly it adds up. And that's just the car costs. What about the whole food-chain thing? When your top predators go extinct, what happens to the balance of nature?

True headline: "Want to Save Money on Car Insurance? Buy a Mountain Lion."

When cougars were reintroduced into South Dakota, something very interesting happened. Insurance claims for deer-vehicle collisions dropped by $1.1 million.[21]

And remember how deer are the deadliest animals in North America (because they cause so many wrecks)? Fewer deer = fewer crashes = fewer human deaths. One research team predicted that if the big cats were reintroduced back into the eastern US, it could prevent 21,400 human injuries, $2.13 billion of repairs, and 155 human deaths.

So, what price do you put on a human life?

✕ ✕ ✕

Mark climbing trees to track pumas and Doug building fences made

---

[21] A single female mountain lion can eat one deer every 16 days. And if she has kittens, she might want one every 3 days. Think how many crashes she's eliminating with each snap of those strong jaws.

sense to me. Their efforts were making a difference. But there are some other not so obvious ways people are helping mountain lions.

Remember P22? Ever since that big cat was spotted by biologist Miguel Ordeñana[22] on the camera traps in Griffith Park, the cat's been a big deal. How do you turn a big deal into a Hollywood sensation? Social media. Thanks to Beth Pratt-Bergstrom and the National Wildlife Federation, P22 now has a Twitter account, a Facebook page, and a movie all about him. Why does he need a following? To raise money. Beth and her crew have started a campaign to build a bridge to help P22 get outta there.[23]

I never thought of building pedestrian bridges for wildlife, but other people have. On Christmas Island in the Indian Ocean, they built bridges for the 50 million or so crabs that move from burrows in the rain forest to the ocean to spawn. Bright red jointed bodies clamber right up metal ramps and skitter across, above the cars. In Singapore, lush jungle trees grow on top of Eco-Link, a bridge arched over 6 lanes of whizzing traffic. Connecting 2 nature preserves, Eco-Link is designed to help banded leaf monkeys, flying lemurs, and pangolins.[24]

---

[22] Imagine being that guy! Miguel was just scrolling through routine deer and coyote pics from their wildlife cameras, hoping for anything exciting, when he skipped right on past the picture the first time. He then froze, carefully clicked back—afraid he might accidentally delete it. Maybe it was just a Great Dane? Maybe he was imagining things? But the size of the tail, the slink of the body, those powerful paws . . . From that moment on, Miguel was frantic to share the good news. A mountain lion right there in his park! Then his job turned into *CSI: Griffith Park*—sniffing out dead deer, piecing together bits of coyote carcass, and tracking down P22's kill sites.

[23] Of course, they could just dart, capture, and move P22, but what about the thousands of other animals trapped in that park. Don't they deserve a route out too?

[24] Pango-whats? Pangolins are the shape of armadillos, with hard fishlike scales covering their body. A pangolin is a mammal who slurps up to 70 million bugs a year with super-sticky spit on a tongue that is longer than the animal's body! A baby pangolin sits on her mommy's tail as she totters safely across the Eco-Link.

In the wide-open spaces of Wyoming, I stood on one of those wildlife-crossing structures. Stooping down, I put my fingers into hoofprints that had dried in the mud, and sniffed piles of droppings left behind. This was evidence that herds of pronghorn[25] and Red Desert mule deer flowed up and over the slicing blade of a road that had severed their ancient migration route. Along that stretch of asphalt, there are now 2 wildlife bridges and 6 underpasses. In the first 3 years, those structures saw 19,290 pronghorn crossings and 40,251 deer crossings. At 150 miles, that Red Desert mule deer migration route is the longest of any mammal in North America. And now this bridge is stitching it back together.

When researchers need to install wildlife bridges and underpasses, how do they know where to put them? They need to know where the roadkill hot spots are. They need data, lots and lots of data, collected by lots and lots of people.

Happy Headlines:

- "Roadkill Warriors Track Carnage to Save Lives"
- "How to Track Road Kill on Your Smart Phone (Seriously)"
- "Roadkill Survey Turns Cyclists into Scientists"

Do you remember Fraser Shilling—the guy who shocked me by saying that if you hit an animal, you should eat it? Over 1,300 volunteers have helped him create the world's largest record of

---

[25] Clocking in at 53 miles per hour, pronghorn are the fastest land animal in North America, but they are still too slow to count on safely crossing roads.

roadkill observations.[26] Observations = data. In San Diego County, when planners needed to know where to install 5 wildlife crossing structures, they called Fraser for access to that critical data.

Every day, everyday citizens are whipping out their smartphones and clicking pics to save animal lives.

Bridges, tunnels, tweets … they aren't the only ways people are putting the brakes on roadkill. All kinds of ideas are being tried out.[27]

More Happy Headlines:

- "Galway 'Bat Bridge' Nearing Completion"[28]
- "Finland: Reflective Reindeer Antlers Aim to
  Stop Accidents"

But wait, there's even more!

I know it sounds like a cheesy infomercial, but I'm so excited, I can't contain myself! As I learned about those amazing advances, it was changing how I saw the future, but what got me super jazzed was when I saw kids making a difference too.

Kids Saving the Rainforest, a group of kids in Costa Rica, realized that the gray-crowned Central American squirrel monkeys were losing their lives crossing roads (or crossing electric lines in order to cross the roads). Those kids didn't just sit around watching it happen. They did something. The kids talked to the

---

[26] That's more than 54,000 observations of 424 different species!

[27] Note: one idea that has been around a long time—whistles on your car to warn deer away—doesn't work. Don't waste your money—or your eardrums.

[28] Just like birds, bats often fly low and right into the path of cars. Bridges guide them to fly up and over the roadway.

electric company. Over the next ten years, they installed 130 blue rope bridges to give the monkeys[29] a safe way across. Thanks in part to the work of these young people, this monkey has been moved from the critically endangered list to the endangered list.

A group of students at Snowflake Junior High in Arizona decided that if drivers knew deer and other big wildlife were near a road, the drivers would slow down. But they realized boring signs wouldn't work. So, for a nationwide STEAM[30] competition run by Samsung, they used a laser cutter to engrave and acid to etch out circuit boards to build a better warning system. When an animal comes close to the road, a solar-powered motion sensor sends a message to a device, and a real-time warning is flashed out. The units cost only $30 each. "If we took just 1/10th of what was spent

---

[29] And at least 11 other species like porcupines, sloths, ants, iguanas, and snakes.
[30] STEAM: Science, Technology, Engineering, Art, and Math.

on wildlife collisions last year," a team spokesperson told me, "we could line both sides of a road with our device from New York all the way to our hometown in Arizona—7 times!"

Their idea was so intriguing, it got passed around the scientific community. A guy in Sweden even commented about it. Oh, and those kids from that little tiny town? Their idea took the regional competition by storm. Then they got to fly to Washington, DC, to go up against schools from across the nation. And their little wildlife–vehicle collision project? It took the competition down.

First place!

The reward? $170,000 for their school district, plus $35,000 to donate to a local nonprofit.[31] Plus, a lifetime of knowing they were changing the world.

What an inspiration.

Kids—in Costa Rica, Arizona, all across the planet—they are my new heroes.

But it's not just those kids on the other side of the globe. Remember those one hundred fifth graders Big Dave was speaking to? Remember the great horned owl's message: "Please don't feed the highway." At the end of the show, Dave turned to the students and said, "Gosh, if one kid goes home and starts telling people, starts spreading that knowledge ... Could you do that for Big Dave?"

Every head in the room nodded.

As Dave swept out of the room with that majestic great horned owl on his arm, I sat back in my chair. That's simple, I thought. We can all stop throwing apple cores out the window. It's not a Hollywood sensation. It's not a cross-country solar-powered

---

[31] They chose the Phoenix Herpetological Society. You know those herps are happy!

motion-sensor warning system. It's not $9 million worth of bridges and tunnels. But it *is* something everyone can do anywhere—everywhere. Even on my little country lane.

Big Dave had just reminded me that simple steps save lives.

I can be part of the solution.

Epilogue

I had decided to not put this story in the book. You see, this particular roadkill didn't lead to any amazing scientific discoveries. There was no scientist waiting eagerly for her tongue tissue. The fur didn't give me a luxurious pelt. Nobody was going to dig parasites out of her lungs. And there surely wasn't anyone setting up Twitter accounts to save this species. Because this was a skunk. Just one little skunk who didn't seem to shine a spotlight on much of anything.

But I was wrong.

This little skunk might, in fact, have taught me the most important lesson of all. But that lesson was so simple, I almost missed it.

It all started when I spotted a black-and-white body at the end of my little country lane—yep, the same lane where the rattler started this whole crazy roadkill obsession. I pulled off to take a sniff.

The odd thing was, the skunk didn't stink. She was dead, head

mashed into the gravel, but she didn't stink. Every other roadkill skunk I had ever found had stunk. Flopping the body over with a stick did not release any of the odor either. Huh. Could there be a skunk who didn't have any odor? Do skunks run out of it? How do they release their stink anyway?

There were fast-food bags littered along the road, enough for this skunk to do her grocery shopping right there.[1] Big Dave's words echoed in my head: *Don't feed the highway.* My day with Doug had me looking around for a wildlife exclusion fence and some kind of underpass, culvert, or *any* way she could have gotten across the road safely.

---

[1] Skunks are omnivores—they eat all kinds of stuff.

Zip, zilch, nada.

I knew it was risky, but I slipped the body into double zipper-lock bags and placed her in my car. She didn't stink, right?

Later, as I tossed her into my basement freezer, I noticed a tiny touch of odor. The next time I opened that door—looking for a spinach-and-mushroom pizza—there was a bit more smell. Nothing you would call stinky . . . just a whiff of burnt tire.

I had always wondered if I could skin a skunk without releasing its essence.[2] Hey, Amber had, right? Before looking at the pelt in her kitchen, I never knew they had gorgeous nails. I had questions: What do those scent sacs look like? How does a skunk make that stuff? Does it have an aimable nozzle?

Every day that little skunk whispered to me from the basement freezer. Taunting me to come find out.

Finally, armed with a skunk anatomy lesson—thanks, internet—and a whole box of rubber gloves, I tied the skunk carcass upside down from a tree branch and held my breath.

Let's just say you *can* skin a skunk without releasing the essence, but that's not what happened. I got the full experience. Even though I'm 100 percent certain I did not nick that scent sac, I soon saw an oily yellow substance ooze out of the skunk's rear end.[3]

It must have started when the rope's knot slipped and the body fell *ker-plunk* on the ground. I guess that forced the scent sac open.

---

[2] "Skunk essence" is what they call it when they sell it. Hunters and trappers use it to mask human scent. Now that's dedication!

[3] In the oil, sulfur compounds called thiols create the raunchy smell. Rotten eggs, sewer gas, farts—they've got sulfur too. The skunk's sticky oil clings to hair, skin, and just about anything else. Then it sinks right in. One study found that humans can smell thiols at 10 parts per billion. That's like if you put all the people from North, South, and Central America in one giant room and only 10 of them had BO but their BO was bad enough to make the whole room stink!

My plan had been to siphon out the essence with a hypodermic needle—the guy in the video made it look so easy.[4] Then I had wanted to cut into the sac itself, to figure out what it was hooked to, to discover where the scent was created. But when that oil crept out—and it started creeping all along the skin, oozing in tiny rivulets and crawling up the hairs—my eyes burned. I began to question my plan. Can it hurt me? Do people go blind from this? Imagine if my face had been sprayed. Do skunk-hunting owls feel this pain?

My nose stung. My eyes leaked as if I had been cutting raw onions for an hour. I could hardly see through all the blinking. When it got so bad that my eyes felt like they were being burned right out of their sockets, I tossed my plan out the window. Why had I thought it would be a good idea to have a vial of vile skunk scent sitting in my office?

I was determined, though, to at least save the pelt. Carefully, carefully, I avoided touching the oily area—it was now the color of dark pee. I kept my fingers and knife far, far away from the ooze, but still somehow, it crept onto me—through double gloves and everything. The odor enveloped me, I had no choice but to inhale

---

[4] Guess I forgot that videos don't include the olfactory.

it, and I knew it was wrapping up in my hair. But I wasn't worried; I had all the ingredients for a neutralizing formula[5] sitting there within reach. But when I was through, even with 3 soaks in that neutralizing formula and lots of scrubbing with 4 different kinds of soap, the smell still clung to me. Plus, I'd made the mistake of going into our house for a few minutes to text some friends that I would *not* be meeting them for dinner. Suddenly, the whole house reeked!

That night, I slept on the porch.

See, there were no big scientific discoveries from that roadkill. I hadn't even really answered my questions. And then, a week later,

---

[5] The recipe is 1 quart hydrogen peroxide, 1/4 cup baking soda, 1 teaspoon dish soap. I think the trick is to use it right away. I must have waited too long.

after the fleshing, pickling, and tanning were all done, when I thought I'd at least have a decent pelt? It still stunk.

And the hair started coming out in clumps.

Disgusted, I gave up.

It wasn't until I started telling people the story of this little skunk that my mind began to change. Friends would ask me about how awful it was; I found myself telling them how amazing it was. Sure, it was inconvenient to have to scrub myself down in the backyard. Sure, my eyes had burned for a while. Sure, my hand still reeked a week later,[6] but I had seen, *really seen*, what makes a skunk such a marvelous creature. This little pipsqueak of an animal has a power so strong that no one dares to mess with her.[7] Now I really knew her power. I had felt it on my flesh, in my eyes, and up my nose.

It was a lot like when I had learned that a rattler had foldable fangs but reading about it wasn't enough. I needed to know it for myself. I hadn't gone through that whole skunky ordeal to get some-*thing*. And it didn't matter that there was no earth-shattering scientific discovery. No. This was about something deeper. This was about *my* curiosity and *my* questions. And they were enough.

---

[6] A skunk doesn't skimp on the stink. In addition to the thiols, her spray has thioacetates, too. Thioacetates aren't too stinky, but they break down very s-l-o-w-l-y, and with the addition of water, they turn into . . . thiols! No wonder it smelled worse every time I washed my hands. Lucky me. I was getting a whole chemistry lesson, too.

[7] Except for, of course, the great horned owl.

SIMPLE ACTS SAVE LIVES

If you're like me, after hearing all these stories, you can't stop thinking about roadkill. So don't! Be an expert, be a scientist, be an animal lover, and do something about it. Here are some ideas, but before you begin any of the projects, ask an adult for permission.

Be an Expert

MORE TO READ

Far Away Fox, Jolene Thompson and Justin Thompson, HMH Books for Young Readers, 2016. Don't let the brief 32 pages of this picture book fool you into thinking it's just fluff. This is a serious story that touches the heart.

Animal Hospital: Rescuing Urban Wildlife, Julia Coey, Firefly Books, 2015. Like the Dodging Death chapter? Want to know more about wildlife rehabilitation? Check out this book (available in paper and digital).

Wild Animal Neighbors: Sharing Our Urban World, Ann Downer, Twenty-First Century Books, 2013. Bears, raccoons, mountain lions living right alongside people in cities? Discover how to create space for wildlife in the concrete jungle.

Migration Nation: Animals on the Go from Coast to Coast, Joanne O'Sullivan, Charlesbridge, 2015. Elephants, manatees, cranes—all animals on the move. Find out more about toad tunnels, frog ferries, and other ways humans are helping mysterious migrators.

When Mountain Lions Are Neighbors: People and Wildlife Working It Out in California, Beth Pratt-Bergstrom, Heyday and the National Wildlife Federation, 2016. This 240-page book was written with adults in mind, but if you care about P22, it will fascinate you.

INTERNET

Kids Saving the Rain Forest: For more on the monkey bridges in Costa Rica: http://www.kidssavingtherainforest.org/monkey-bridge -program.html.

Science News for Students: Roadkill: Learning from the dead. Read this article for a closer look at how paleontologist Dr. Michelle Stocker gathers and prepares squished specimens to help her study dinosaurs: https://www.sciencenewsforstudents.org/article/roadkill -learning-dead.

Roadkill Skeletons: Check out skeletons rebuilt from roadkill by young Francois Malherbe in South Africa: http://www.roadkillskeletons.co .za/.

Jake's Bones: Fourteen-year-old Jake McGowan-Lowe has been collecting and cleaning bones since he was six. His blog has all the gory details: http://www.jakes-bones.com/.

VIDEOS

"Why This Museum Stores Thousands of Dead Animals in Its Freezer": Want to watch museum staff process roadkill specimens? This National Geographic video is for you: http://video.nationalgeographic .com/video/news/160803-news-salvage-animals-vin.

Roadkill experiment: Mark Rober explains his simple scientific experiment to see which animal people hit most often: https://www .youtube.com/watch?v=k-Fp7flAWMA.

Animex Wildlife Bridge: BBC put together this 5-minute video on bridges that one company built for the adorable little hazel dormouse: https://www.youtube.com/watch?v=FVy5R1WR-iY&sns=em.

Five Crazy Bridges for Animals: a 2-minute video that sums up big ideas about how humans unintentionally create barriers for animals: https://www.youtube.com/watch?v=VjCJvn__N5c.

The Cat That Changed America: a brief video about P22, the Hollywood mountain lion celebrity: https://www.youtube.com/watch?v=kdf_fr FSogM.

Be a Scientist

Bumper Bugs: Does picking through body parts sound like a whole lot of awesome? Do you like piecing together puzzles? Want to get hands-on with all this science? A car might be the perfect research instrument for you!

Fire Up the Grille

1. Find someone who owns a car and ask if you can study bug parts from the grille of the car.
2. Gather your gear: plastic container (e.g., yogurt cup), tweezers, magnifying glass, white paper, journal, pencil, insect field guide or access to the internet.
3. Gently remove any bug parts from the grille of the vehicle and put them in the container. Be careful not to scratch the paint!
4. Spread the body parts on white paper and try to piece them together. Use the guidebook or the internet to try to identify your bugs.
5. What questions do you have? Write them down. Make labeled sketches to record your findings. Don't forget the date, location, and names of anyone on your research team.

Critter Counts

You can conduct your own roadkill surveys by recording insect data.

1. Ask a car owner for permission. Using a soft cloth or squeegee, scrub the windshield clean.
2. Record the vehicle's mileage before a trip. After the trip, record the new mileage, the date, the weather conditions, and the route of the trip. Calculate and record the length of the trip.

3. Sit inside the car and make a sketch of the windshield (if there are lots of bug splatters, limit your study to half or a quarter of the window).
4. Mark every bug splatter you see and label with data such as color, size, description, type of insect (if you can tell). Record your data in a chart so that you can compare it to later trips.
5. What questions come to mind? Are more insects killed during certain months? Does the number of splatters vary based on the habitat driven through? Can you devise a test to answer your questions?

I want to know what you find out! Report your research at www.HeatherLMontgomery.com.

Citizen Scientists Projects

Get active with larger science projects. Some projects are specific to a certain location, some use apps, some request digital photos, and some use good old paper and pencil. Be careful: certain projects are not safe for young people. To find the perfect project for you, search the internet for "Roadkill citizen science." Or check out one of these:

Walking, running, or biking? Join the Adventure Scientists project at http://www.adventurescience.org/.
Check out the SciGirls Citizen science project search, http://pbskids.org/scigirls/citizen-science, or the adult version at SciStarter, https://scistarter.com/finder, and search for "roadkill."
Visit http://www.inaturalist.org/projects and type "roadkill" into the search box. You may want to add your state or country name to narrow down your search.
Go to the app store on your device and find an app that tracks roadkill in your area.

Dig around and find a project you love, then get busy saving lives!

Be an Animal Lover

Get the word out: How can you use your words to change the world? Thirteen-year-old Olivia Ries blogs for Nat Geo. For inspiration, read her article about monkey bridges: https://blog.education.national geographic.com/2016/05/18/monkey-bridges-for-everyone/.

Put your money where your mouth is: if you care about animals, you can donate money to groups who are working to prevent animal-vehicle collisions. Do chores or odd jobs, or find other ways to earn the money.

Simple acts save lives: make a list of things you can do in your daily life to help wildlife. Ideas to start with:

- With an adult, go pick up litter.
- Encourage drivers to go slowly, especially at dusk and dawn. Tip: this may mean you need to leave earlier!
- Teach your friends Big Dave's message: *don't feed the highway.*

ANNOTATED BIBLIOGRAPHY

For this book, I did all kinds of research: elbow-deep-in-the-compost research, microphone-in-hand research, musty-stack-of-books research, I-can't-understand-your-language research, keep-you-up-till-midnight research . . .

I only wish that years ago I had *gotten it* about research. About how much fun it is. Think about how much time I've wasted being okay with "good enough" answers. If you are like me and want to dig deeper, here are some of the most interesting sources I found. Want to see the whole list? Visit HeatherLMontgomery.com.

Maybe these will ignite your questions and inspire you to tear into something kind of rotten that's just waiting to explode with discovery.

A Note from Me

Martill, Tischlinger & Longrich. 2015. "A Four-Legged Snake from the Early Cretaceous of Gondwana." *Science.* http://dx.doi.org/10.1126/science.aaa9208.

That four-legged snake controversy? As scientist David Martill was walking through a museum in Germany, his jaw dropped. The cause? An "unknown" fossil with a snaking body and both front and back legs. No four-legged snakes had ever been found. David just *knew* it was a snake. His article stirred up a whole slippery, slithering set of questions and controversy.

Kennedy, Merrit. "How Snakes Lost Their Legs." NPR, 20 Oct. 2016. Web. 25 July 2017. http://www.npr.org/sections/thetwo-way/2016/10/20/498575639/how-snakes-lost-their-legs.

If you're interested in more about the spurs on pythons, National Public Radio did this great little article and video about it.

Stewart, Will. "Bubonic Plague Terror." *The Sun.* News Group Newspapers Limited, 14 July 2016. Web. 6 July 2017.

https://www.thesun.co.uk/news/1442838/bubonic-plague-mass
-vaccinations-ordered-in-russia-after-boy-is-struck-down-by
-horrific-disease-that-wiped-out-half-of-europe/.
I had no personal experience with what bad things you can catch
from dead animals—am I careful or just lucky? So I cast my research
net out onto the World Wide Web. Never did I dream it could be as
bad as that bubonic plague nightmare. Keep your hands clean—we
don't need to see that again!

Chapter 1: Rattled

This chapter is based on my personal experiences. The best kind of
research IMHO. But to understand the science behind snakes and
venom, I dug into textbooks and heavy-duty science articles.

Palermo, Elizabeth. "Can a Severed Snake Head Still Kill? It's Possible."
    LiveScience. Purch, 30 Aug. 2014. Web. 22 Mar. 2017. http://www
    .livescience.com/47626-severed-snake-head-can-still-bite.html.
    There are lots of crazy stories about snakes out there, so you never
    know which ones to trust. I loved this article, which quoted a
    biology professor and explained just why after-death reflexes are
    stronger in snakes than other carnivores. It was from a source
    I trusted, it included information from a reliable expert, and the
    facts made sense.
Levin, Ted. *America's Snake: The Rise and Fall of the Timber
    Rattlesnake*. Chicago: U of Chicago, 2016. Print.
    Every cool thing you ever wanted to know about timber
    rattlesnakes!
Binns, Corey. "How Do Snakes Swallow Large Animals?" *LiveScience*.
    Purch, 11 Sept. 2012. Web. 15 June 2017. https://www.livescience
    .com/32096-how-do-snakes-swallow-large-animals.html.
    With a video of one snake eating another (and vomiting it back up!).

Chapter 2: Library of Life

David Laurencio at the Auburn University Museum of Natural History was such a great teacher. His words, as well as the day I spent with Melissa Miller, formed the core of this chapter.

"Python Elimination Program." South Florida Water Management District. N.p., n.d. Web. 11 July 2017. https://www.sfwmd.gov/our -work/python-program.
From this website, I learned about the vast numbers of pythons being eradicated. Check it out to see how they stack up to the Empire State Building.
Miller, Melissa A., John M. Kinsella, Ray W. Snow, Malorie M. Hayes, Bryan Falk, Robert N. Reed, Frank J. Mazzotti, Craig Guyer, and Christina M. Romagosa. "Parasite Spillover or Spillback? Identifying the Origin of Pentastome Parasites of Invasive Burmese Pythons in the Florida Everglades." Diss. Auburn U, 2017. Print.
Melissa was kind enough to share an early draft of her dissertation with me, so those facts are as fresh as you can get. See, this is why real research is cool—you get to know stuff before the rest of the scientific community does!

Chapter 3: Dead Discoveries

Dr. Bridgett vonHoldt's telephone interview blew me away, so much so that I ended it early to go look this stuff up and recover from my not-so-rational reaction.

"Frequently Asked Questions." Turkey Vulture Society. N.p., n.d. Web. 25 July 2017. https://turkeyvulturesociety.wordpress.com/quick -facts/frequently-asked-questions/.

Got questions about these bald-headed, leg-pooping birds? The
Turkey Vulture Society has got you covered.

Bergman, Stevie, and Bridgett vonHoldt. "Bridgett VonHoldt on
Epigenetics, Molecular Ecology, and Canine Domestication." *These
Vibes Are Too Cosmic*. WPRB Princeton 103.3, 04 Oct. 2016. Web. 17
July 2017. https://tvr2c.com/2016/10/05/10416-show-feat-bridgett
-vonholdt-on-epigenetics-molecular-ecology-and-canine
-domestication/.

It's always a good idea to learn more about your sources, their biases
and background—especially when someone's making claims that
might be controversial. I did some snooping around on Dr. vonHoldt.
Her position at Princeton, her previous publications, and this audio
interview gave me more confidence in the soundness of Bridgett's
science. The tidbit that she's a cat person made her come alive.

"Objectives." Princeton University. The Trustees of Princeton
University, n.d. Web. 17 July 2017. http://canineancestry.princeton
.edu/project.html.

Learn all about Bridgett's Canine Ancestry Project and scroll in on
the map to see the black coyote's data point! It's the only one in
Alabama so far, but I'm working on changing that.

Head, Vernon R. L. *The Rarest Bird in the World: The Search for the
Nechisar Nightjar*. Pegasus, 2016. Print.

A whole book on the discovery of that nightjar from 1 wing of a roadkill.

Chapter 4: Roadkill Counts

Scientific papers supplied the bulk of the information for this fact-filled
chapter. I've included just a sampling of those below along with some
other fun resources.

Motley, Jeremy L., Blake W. Stamps, Carter A. Mitchell, Alec T.
Thompson, Jayson Cross, Jianlan You, Douglas R. Powell,

Bradley S. Stevenson, and Robert H. Cichewicz. "Opportunistic
Sampling of Roadkill As an Entry Point to Accessing Natural
Products Assembled by Bacteria Associated with Non-Anthropoidal
Mammalian Microbiomes." *Journal of Natural Products* 80.3 (2016):
598–608. American Chemical Society and American Society of
Pharmacognosy. Web. 21 July 2017.

If you are interested in how to sample bacteria from opossum
roadkill—and laser ablation electrospray ionization mass
spectrometry, bioassay testing, and metabolites such as cyclic
lipodepsipeptides.

"Dog Raises a Baby Opossum After Its Mother Was Killed by a Car."
Amazing Animals. Rare Species Fund, 5 Jan. 2015. Web. 6 July 2017.
https://www.youtube.com/watch?v=QeIxWVkviOQ.

For more on the endearing story of Hantu and his adopted possum,
Poncho.

Adams, Sheila, and Brewster Bartlett. "Making Connections Webcast
Show #29: Roadkill Project." *Roadkill 2012.* EdTechTalk, 19 Feb. 2008.
Web. 6 July 2017. http://roadkill.edutel.com/rkabout.html.

What do teachers do after school? They get on webcasts and talk to
other teachers about the best science projects for students!

United States of America. U.S. Department of Transportation. Federal
Highway Administration. *Wildlife-Vehicle Collision Reduction Study:
Report to Congress.* By M. P. Huijser, P. McGowen, J. Fuller, A. Hardy,
A. Kociolek, A. P. Clevenger, D. Smith, and R. Ament. N.p.: Federal
Highway Administration, 2008. Web. 4 Apr. 2017. https://www.fhwa
.dot.gov/publications/research/safety/08034/08034.pdf.

Just where did I learn that porcupines lick roads for salt? Smack
dab in the middle of this 232-page government report.

Dell'Amore, Christine. "Amazing Video: Inside the World's Largest
Gathering of Snakes." *National Geographic.* National Geographic
Society, n.d. Web. 13 Apr. 2017. http://news.nationalgeographic.com
/news/2014/06/140626-snakes-narcisse-animals-mating-sex
-animals-world/.

Love the river of snakes that migrates to one spot in Canada? This is the video for you.

Ree, Rodney van der, Daniel J. Smith, and Clara Grilo. *Handbook of Road Ecology*. Chichester, West Sussex: John Wiley & Sons, 2015. Print.
This is *the book* for all the best data on roadkill and mitigation efforts across the globe. I used this textbook for numbers on how many large mammals become roadkill every year, info about bighorn sheep licking roads, and additional details about hyena tails being used for traditional medicine.

Rober, Mark. "Turtles or Snakes—Which Do Cars Hit More? ROADKILL EXPERIMENT." YouTube. 19 July 2012. Web. 05 Apr. 2017. https://www.youtube.com/watch?v=k-Fp7flAWMA.
Scientific method, data collection, and analysis all in one short humorous video—plus a sobering conclusion and a quick look at people who stopped to help the wildlife.

Chapter 5: On the Trail of Dead Devils

For my Skype interview with Dr. Elizabeth Murchison, I prepared like I do for all interviews. I watched her TED Talk, read articles about Tasmanian devils, and plowed through her scientific papers. I had a list of questions ready, but when we got on the call, she made it easy. It was like talking to an old friend!

Murchison, Elizabeth. "Fighting a Contagious Cancer." *Elizabeth Murchison: Fighting a Contagious Cancer*. TED Talk. TED.com. July 2011. Web. 22 Mar. 2017. https://www.ted.com/talks/elizabeth_murchison.
To see what I mean about Elizabeth's enthusiasm, watch this talk. But fair warning: the pics of the tumors are gross and graphic.

Jabr, Ferris. "Will Cloning Ever Save Endangered Animals?" *Scientific American*. Scientific American, 11 Mar. 2013. Web. 12 July 2017.

https://www.scientificamerican.com/article/cloning-endangered
-animals/.
This article poses a really good question. What do you think?

Brookshire, Bethany. "Roadkill: Learning from the Dead." *Science News for Students*. Society for Science and the Public, 18 Feb. 2016. Web. 10 Aug. 2017. https://www.sciencenewsforstudents.org/article /roadkill-learning-dead.
I emailed, interviewed, and read Dr. Stocker's scientific papers. They're pretty cool and very technical. This website gives a great kid-friendly version.

Chapter 6: Please Pass the Salt

Obviously, this chapter's all about the hands-on research. When I processed that fox pelt, I didn't know I'd be writing a book about it. The notes and greasy splotches in my nature journal reminded me of all the gruesome details.

"Hair Slippage." *Van Dyke's Taxidermy*. A McKenzie Company, n.d. Web. 17 July 2017. https://www.vandykestaxidermy.com/Hair -Slippage-W50.aspx.
Curious about hair slippage and other not-so-polite details of taxidermy? Van Dyke's is the place to find it all.

Trail Kids Happy Trails. "Roadkill Skeletons: Reconstructing a Giant." YouTube, 20 July 2015. Web. 18 July 2017. https://www.youtube.com /watch?v=IisipV9iDrk.
You don't want to miss this video showing Francois reconstructing the giraffe!

Gade, Gene. "The Ancient and Arduous Art of Brain Tanning Buffalo Hides." N.p., n.d. Vore Buffalo Jump Foundation. Web. 12 July 2017. http://www.vorebuffalojump.org/pdf/VBJF%20 Brain%20tanning.pdf.

Finding a scientific explanation for brain tanning was tough. I think that when many writers don't understand the material themselves, they kind of skip over the explanation. I was grateful to Gene Gade, who, in this newsletter article, explained what he could and then admitted that the biochemistry of the process is not totally understood.

Chapter 7: Rogue Taxidermy

Talk about helpful! Amber Maykut let me go right into her home for our interview. At that point, she had no idea if I intended to write a scathing review or a glowing story about her unique profession. I'm so thankful for her openness and passion that let me see through my prejudice. I'm glad to hear that her business, Brooklyn Taxidermy (https://www .brooklyntaxidermy.com), and classes are booming these days.

Collinson, Wendy. "The Uses of Roadkill!" *Roadkill Research*. N.p., 13 Oct. 2011. Web. 17 July 2017. https://roadkillresearch.wordpress .com/2011/10/13/the-uses-of-roadkill/.
  When I was just starting on my research journey, Wendy Collinson of South Africa gave me an interview and set the stage for much of my research. She connected me with road ecologists, shared her fascinating newsletters (like this one, which shows hats, games, and other bizarre uses of roadkill), and opened my eyes to the international scope of this issue.
Warner, Sam. "These Men Turn Your Dead Pets into Drones." *Digital Spy*. Hearst Magazines, 30 July 2016. Web. 17 July 2017. http://www .digitalspy.com/tech/news/a803115/these-men-turn-your-dead-pets -into-drones/.
  I know you want to see that drone roadkill in action. Video included. Warning: in my research I avoided looking at pets hit by cars. These guys don't.

"Photobucket." Photobucket.com. N.p., n.d. Web. 14 June 2017. http://
photobucket.com/gallery/http://s178.photobucket.com/user
/chachimac/media/squirrelfoosballtable.jpg.html.
Photo bucket as a reference? Yes. Creepy Foosball table made of
rodents. See how much fun research is?

Chapter 8: Oh Deer!

This chapter is full of squirm-inducing research. At first I refused to
consider this topic, but I'm so glad I did! Interviewing Crystal Sands
helped to change my mind.

Brand, John. "Space Farms Wins Roadkill Removal Bid." *New Jersey
Herald*. Quincy Media, 30 Aug. 2006. Web. 17 July 2017. http://www
.njherald.com/article/20060830/ARTICLE/308309967#.
To figure out if zoos feeding their animals roadkill was just a myth,
I looked for reliable references. The *New Jersey Herald* published
this article with enough plausible detail to convince me. Gas hissing
out of a bloated deer belly? I've witnessed that myself.
Bonhotal, Jean, Ellen Z. Harrison, and Mary Schwarz. "Composting
Road Kill." (2007): n.p. Cornell Waste Management Institute.
Cornell Cooperative Extension, 2007. Web. 16 June 2017. http://
cwmi.css.cornell.edu/roadkillfs.pdf.
I got to interview Mary Schwarz, who helped to develop, refine, and
train others to use the deer-composting method. She's a total
believer—she's composted her pet dog and wants her own body to
be composted.
"The Man Who Eats Roadkill." Dir. Nick Ahlmark. Perf. Arthur Boyt.
YouTube. Vice Fringes. Vice Video, 15 Mar. 2013. Web. 16 June 2017.
https://www.youtube.com/watch?v=OQvt-gxbq5E.
This video is outrageous, but I'm including it because I know you
want to watch Arthur Boyt chow down on badger brains.

Johnson, Kirk. "Laurie the Moose Lady Puts 'Heart and Soul' into Roadkill." *New York Times*, 26 Aug. 2016. Web. 17 July 2017. https://www.nytimes.com/2016/08/27/us/laurie-the-moose-lady -puts-heart-and-soul-into-roadkill.html#whats-next.
Want more on the Alaska story? Me too. Here's an article on a volunteer who hauls roadkill to feed the hungry.

Chapter 9: Mama

Personal experience is often the best kind of research. It can also be the most troubling, but scientists and writers push through those emotions and dig deeper to learn everything they can from each experience.

Steen, D.A., J.P. Gibbs, K.A. Buhlmann, J.L. Carr, B.W. Compton, J.D. Congdon, J.S. Doody, J.C. Godwin, K.L. Holcomb, D.R. Jackson, F.J. Janzen, G. Johnson, M.T. Jones, J.T. Lamer, T.A. Langen, M.V. Plummer, J.W. Rowe, R.A. Saumure, J.K. Tucker, and D.S. Wilson. "Terrestrial Habitat Requirements of Nesting Freshwater Turtles." *Biological Conservation* 150.1 (2012): 121–28. Web. 15 July 2017. http:// www.harding.edu/plummer/pdf/steenetal2012.pdf.
Mean, median, standard deviation? If you wonder why you have to learn math when all you want to do is study animals, check out Dr. Steen's research. Skip down to Table 1, and you'll see why I appreciate my math teachers.
"How to Help a Snapping Turtle Cross the Road." YouTube. Toronto Zoo, 05 Oct. 2010. Web. 15 July 2017. https://www.youtube.com /watch?v=Lgd_B6iKPxU.
The *right* way to move a turtle across the road.
Steen, David A. "Why I Gave Mouth-to-Mouth Resuscitation to a Turtle." *Slate Magazine*. 10 Sept. 2014. Web. 15 July 2017. http://www .slate.com/blogs/wild_things/2014/09/10/turtle_cpr_scientist _gives_mouth_to_mouth_resuscitation_video.html?wpsrc=sh_all _dt_tw_top.

I thought you'd be looking for more about that mouth-to-mouth resuscitation. Too cool!

Chapter 10: Dodging Death

From teaching me how to assess a raptor's health from its keel to giving me the greatest gift of releasing a red-tailed hawk, Katie, Scottie, and Doug showed me the true power of rehabilitation. I'll be forever grateful to them for that experience. Learn more, get involved, or support their important work at https://www.awrc.org/.

Chapter 11: Trees, Tolls, and Tweets

Doug Feremenga, Fraser Shilling, and all the professionals at the roadkill conference (formally known as the International Conference on Ecology and Transportation) opened my eyes to the amazing work being done. Many interviews informed this chapter.

"Capturing Florida Panthers." The Florida Panther. Florida Fish and Wildlife Conservation Commission, n.d. Web. 07 Sept. 2017. http://myfwc.com/wildlifehabitats/managed/panther/capture/. Watch Mark Lotz and crew collar a panther.
"P-22 Mountain Lion." National Wildlife Federation, n.d. Web. 09 Oct. 2017. https://www.nwf.org/en/Save-LA-Cougars/P22-Mountain-Lion. Get to know P22!
McFall, Valarie, T. Winston Vickers, Doug Feremenga, and Patrick Huber. Poster. Proc. of International Conference on Ecology & Transportation, North Carolina, Raleigh. Transportation Corridor Agencies, UC Davis Veterinary Medicine, 2015. Web. 9 Oct. 2017. http://www.thetollroads.com/sites/default/files/pdf/icoet_poster.pdf. This poster provides a great summary of the fence project in California.

"KSTR Spokeskids Talking about the Titi Monkeys." YouTube. Kids Saving the Rainforest, 23 Mar. 2013. Web. 18 July 2017. https://www.youtube.com/watch?v=Cn2GV16ymu0&feature=c4-overview&list=UUj_nOjRTfmjI1nH7x4arErw.

Just how do you get info on a project halfway around the world from you? YouTube!

"Samsung Solve for Tomorrow—Snowflake Junior High School." Samsung Electronics America. N.p., n.d. Web. 10 Aug. 2017. http://www.samsung.com/us/solvefortomorrow/home.html.

Those kids who won the national championship? Check out their low-cost deer detection system project!

ACKNOWLEDGMENTS

This book belongs to the super scientists, conservationists, and citizens who spend their lives paying attention to roadkill. I simply recorded their stories. In addition to David, Melissa, Bridgett, Elizabeth, Michelle, Francois, Donnie, Amber, Fraser, Tom, Crystal, Doug, Scottie, and Katie, whose interviews made it into the book, dozens of others fed me delicious information and roadkill stories. Thank you.

There are plenty of facts in this book, but there is bias, too. You see, I chose which facts and stories to include. All errors are my own.

The way I told the story was influenced by the many writers I've read. In particular, the works of Mary Roach, Georgia Bragg, and Sy Montgomery showed me new possibilities, and I am indebted to them for opening my mind.

My thanks go to my friend Pam, who first taught me why I shouldn't toss my apple core out the window. The school librarians of Tennessee Association of School Librarians (TASL), who showed me that everyone enjoys a good rattlesnake roadkill story. Carolyn, who encouraged me when I was scared of this topic. Janice, who helped me wrestle with tough topics. My nature retreat buddies, Jodi and Lisa. Aunt Paula, who told me I could do anything I set my mind to. My NF Kidlit discussion group; my beta readers: Candice, Hilarie, Jodi, Norma, and Susannah; and critique group friends: Annie Laura, Bonnie, Chrysantha, Darren, Jared, Mark, Mary Kay, Melanie, Nancy, Nellie, Patty, Shanda, and Tina. I couldn't have done it without you all!

This research would have never become the book it is without the Southern Breeze region of the Society of Children's Book Writers and Illustrators and the sage guidance of Rubin Pfeffer, who led me to Susan Dobinick. Thank you, Susan, for falling in love with a quirky manuscript, asking perceptive questions, and giving this story a chance to be heard. The animals and I owe the entire team at Bloomsbury our deepest appreciation for their support.

INDEX

Note: The letter n after page numbers refers to footnotes and is followed by the note number.

HEATHER L. MONTGOMERY is wild about animals. Some things that make her curious: petrified body parts, tree guts, and weirdo insects. Heather has taught inside and outside the classroom, directed an environmental center, and led thousands of kids on outdoor adventures. She spends her free time climbing trees, exploring the wilderness, and playing with her dog, Piper. Heather lives near Ardmore, Alabama.

heatherlmontgomery.com

KEVIN O'MALLEY is the illustrator of *How They Croaked* and the coauthor and illustrator of the popular Miss Malarkey series, the *New York Times* bestseller *Gimme Cracked Corn and I Will Share*, and many other books for children. He lives in Maryland.

booksbyomalley.com

STRESS LESS COLORING:
LOVE

100+ COLORING PAGES FOR FUN AND RELAXATION

A adamsmedia

Avon, Massachusetts

Published by
Adams Media, a division of F+W Media, Inc.
57 Littlefield Street, Avon, MA 02322. U.S.A.
www.adamsmedia.com

Contains material adapted from *The Everything® Stress Management Book* by Eve Adamson, copyright © 2002 by F+W Media, Inc., ISBN 10: 1-58062-578-9, ISBN 13: 978-1-58062-578-4.

ISBN 10: 1-4405-9592-5
ISBN 13: 978-1-4405-9592-9

Printed in the United States of America.

10   9   8   7   6   5   4   3   2

This book is intended as general information only, and should not be used to diagnose or treat any health condition. In light of the complex, individual, and specific nature of health problems, this book is not intended to replace professional medical advice. The ideas, procedures, and suggestions in this book are intended to supplement, not replace, the advice of a trained medical professional. Consult your physician before adopting any of the suggestions in this book, as well as about any condition that may require diagnosis or medical attention. The author and publisher disclaim any liability arising directly or indirectly from the use of this book.

Many of the designations used by manufacturers and sellers to distinguish their products are claimed as trademarks. Where those designations appear in this book and F+W Media, Inc. was aware of a trademark claim, the designations have been printed with initial capital letters.

Cover design by Stephanie Hannus.
Cover images © iStockphoto.com/AlenaSalanovich; iStockphoto.com/alecsia.

This book is available at quantity discounts for bulk purchases.
For information, please call 1-800-289-0963.

INTRODUCTION

Looking to relax? Want to feel more creative? Need more peace and quiet in your life?

If you're looking to get rid of all the extra stress in your life, just pick up a pencil, crayon, or marker and let *Stress Less Coloring: Love* help you manage your worries in a fun, easy, therapeutic way.

Over the years, studies have shown that coloring allows your mind to concentrate solely on the task at hand, which brings you into a restful state similar to what you can achieve through meditation. When you allow yourself to focus on the creative artwork in front of you, your mind doesn't have room for all the anxiety and stress in your life. And when your mind relaxes, your body follows, by letting go of any tension and giving you a sense of peace and well-being.

Throughout the book, you'll find more than 100 black-and-white prints depicting a variety of beautiful love designs that are just waiting to be colored in. And the beauty of these prints is that you can color them in however you'd like. The most relaxing colors are cool shades such as greens, blues, and purples, but if you'd rather splash bold, bright hues like red, yellow, or orange across the page, feel free! Let your own unique palette guide your hand and personalize your pattern.

So whether you're new to art therapy or have been embracing the fun of coloring for years, it's time to stress less and find your inner calm and creativity—one love print at a time.

I LOVE YOU